Hamlet

(Study Guide)

Hamlet - A William Shakespeare Play, with Study Guide

(Literature Unpacked)

Eleanor Henderson

INTRODUCTION

Besides "Romeo and Juliet," "The Tragedy of Hamlet, Prince of Denmark" is probably Will Shakespeare's most studied and performed stage play. Nowadays, it's simply called "Hamlet."

The titular character is also the role every actor aspires to portray. Having played Hamlet is considered the pinnacle of an acting career. This is due to how Shakespeare created a story and main character so nuanced, so profound, that these have continuously fascinated us for centuries. The play is considered one of the most influential classics of world literature.

PLOT SUMMARY

Hamlet, the Prince of Denmark, comes home from his studies abroad to find that, after the untimely death of his father the (also named Hamlet), his mother Queen Gertrude has already married his father's brother Claudius, who has been crowned the new King. On top of this, the neighboring Prince of Norway, Fortinbras, plans to invade Denmark as punishment for the death of his own father some years back, who was killed by Hamlet's father.

Meanwhile, Hamlet's best friend Horatio, and the watchmen of Castle Elsinore witness the nightly haunting of the ghost of old King Hamlet at the battlements. When they tell Hamlet about it, he joins the watch to witness the haunting himself. The ghost begs Hamlet to avenge his murder by Claudius.

Hamlet is at first shocked and filled with vengeful thoughts at this revelation; he is resolved to pretend he is a mad fool hide his plans for revenge from everyone at court. But as the days pass, he wavers in his resolve. He wonders at the possible outcomes of acting on his need for vengeance, versus inaction and staying safe. Apart from Horatio, he is not sure he can trust anyone – not his old schoolmates Rosencrantz and Guildenstern, not his uncle Claudius nor his mother Gertrude, and not even Ophelia, the girl he loves, as he suspects her father Polonius is using her to spy on him. The situation nearly drives him completely mad. He also wonders if what the ghost revealed was the truth.

To discover the truth of Claudius's guilt, Hamlet hires a company of traveling actors, and instructs them to perform a play about the usurpation of a king by his brother, at court, in the presence of King Claudius and Queen Gertrude.

Upon beholding the play, Claudius becomes upset and storms out of the scene, and goes into a private area to kneel and pray. Hamlet becomes convinced of his uncle's guilt, and almost kills him. But when Hamlet sees him at prayer, he relents, unwilling to turn his uncle into a holy martyr. He rushes to his mother's room instead and confronts her with his suspicions about her adultery.

Ophelia's father, Polonius, eavesdrops on their argument. When Gertrude cries out, thinking that Hamlet is about to kill her, Polonius cries out as well, giving himself away. Hamlet runs his sword through Polonius's hiding place, mistaking him for the Claudius, and inadvertently kills him. Hamlet discovers his error. In his moment of anguish, the ghost of old King Hamlet appears before him, but remains invisible to Gertrude. As Hamlet converses with the ghost, Gertrude becomes convinced that Hamlet has gone mad.

Claudius takes the situation as an opportunity to exile Hamlet to England (officially, for killing Polonius and for having gone insane), accompanied by Hamlet's schoolmates, Rozencrantz and Guildenstern. But Claudius sends them with sealed written request for the King of England to execute Hamlet. However, Hamlet manages to outwit Claudius's plans by switching the sealed letter with another one telling the King of England to execute his schoolmates instead, and escapes back to Denmark.

Meanwhile, Ophelia becomes demented with grief over her father Polonius's death, and eventually dies from drowning in a brook in an apparent suicide. Her brother Laertes swears to avenge his father and sister, and issues Hamlet a challenge. Claudius persuades Laertes to kill Hamlet with a poison-tipped sword, in a seemingly civil sword fight at court to settle their differences. In case Laertes would lose the fight, Claudius would have a poisoned victory drink prepared for Hamlet.

Hamlet accepts the challenge, unaware of Claudius's plan. On the day of the fight at court, Hamlet proves to be the better fighter at first, and Queen Gertrude proudly drinks to her son's seemingly imminent triumph – using the poisoned cup of wine. Realizing that only he can kill Hamlet now, a desperate Laertes scores a hit on Hamlet with the poisoned sword while he is off-guard. Enraged, Hamlet scuffles with him, grabs Laertes's poisoned sword, and wounds him with it as well.

The queen dies. As Laertes dies from the poison, he reveals Claudius's whole plot to Hamlet. Before he himself dies, Hamlet finally decides to kill Claudius by ramming the poisoned sword into him, and forcing him to drink the rest of the poisoned wine. With his dying breath, Hamlet declares Prince Fortinbras of Norway as the successor to the Danish throne, and bids his friend Horatio to tell his story.

CHARACTERS

"Hamlet" actually has 35 speaking roles, both major and minor characters, plus an unspecified number of non-speaking extras as lords, ladies, officers, soldiers, sailors, and servants. We shall focus only on the most important characters.

Important Major Characters

Hamlet

The titular Prince of Denmark is young, charismatic, sensitive, impulsive, philosophical, and greatly troubled. He is forced to deal with the deadly politics of his country and the dysfunction in his own family. Hamlet spends much of his energy agonizing over his next action should be. He is no longer a boy. But while he remains indecisive, he is not yet a man, either. Ironically, the moment he becomes a man and decides to exact justice on Claudius, is also the moment he must die.

Claudius

He is the power-hungry man who killed his brother, King Hamlet. But we spend the better half of the play wondering just how evil he truly is. When he kneels in prayer, we wonder if he repents his sin; when he sends the King of England the request to execute Hamlet, we wonder if it's just a desperate attempt to defend himself from Hamlet's dangerous behaviour. But all doubts melt away when Claudius conspires with Laertes to have Hamlet killed in a traitorous fashion.

Polonius

He is the slightly annoying Lord Chamberlain who tries his best to ingratiate himself to King Claudius by spying on Hamlet's activities. He succeeds in destroying the growing relationship between his daughter Ophelia and Prince Hamlet. He actually has limited political power at court, but the manner by which he advises Claudius and Gertrude implies that he thinks he has great influence.

Gertrude

She is Hamlet's enigmatic mother. She is an interesting character, for even as she speaks does not give voice to her innermost thoughts or secrets. We never really know where she stands on the moral spectrum. We never find out if she plotted against King Hamlet or not, or if she had an adulterous affair with Claudius while King Hamlet still lived. We don't even know how much she loved her son Hamlet. Shakespeare leaves a lot about her ambiguous, on purpose.

Ophelia

She is Polonius's pretty, innocent daughter. Her life is greatly controlled by her father and the world around her. The political situation she and Hamlet are in makes it impossible for trust and love to grow further between them. Polonius makes her sever ties with Hamlet, and she tries her best to comply. But once she loses Hamlet's trust and he kills her father, grief and deep-seated anger at the people around her drive her insane.

Important Minor Characters

Ghost of King Hamlet – This is the phantom that haunts the ramparts of Elsinore, and Prince Hamlet's mind. While the ghost's first appearance is obviously a vision shared by Hamlet, Horatio, and the other members of the castle guard, at other times the ghost seems to be a part of Hamlet's psyche.

Horatio – Hamlet's best friend is a practical and earthbound soul. He acts as a foil to Hamlet's mercurial presence. But he ultimately proves to be the one trustworthy person Hamlet has left in his life.

Laertes – Like Hamlet, he is young and impulsive. But unlike Hamlet, he can sustain rage long enough to plot someone's murder – in this case, Hamlet's.

Rosencrantz and Guildenstern – Hamlet's former schoolmates and members of the Danish court, they are opportunistic young men. They are willing to engage in intrigue and to spy on their comrade Hamlet, if it brings social advancement for themselves.

Gravediggers – Two clownish fellows whose job it is to clear out old graves for new ones. One of the graves they dig out is that of old Yorick, the late King Hamlet's court jester. They provide comic relief in an otherwise morbid scene.

HISTORICAL CONTEXT

To better appreciate the depth of meaning in the play, it's a good idea to know both the historical context of "Hamlet" the play, and of the time in which William Shakespeare wrote it.

Turn-of-the-century culture

There is no certain date for when William Shakespeare wrote "Hamlet." Based on existing historical evidence, scholars estimate it was written sometime between 1599 – because "Hamlet" mentions another Shakespeare play, "Julius Caesar," first produced in 1599 – and 1602, when the earliest production of "Hamlet" was recorded within the register of a London livery company or trade association.

The years 1599 to 1602 also mark the last few years of England's most illustrious female monarch, Queen Elizabeth I. (She would die of natural causes in 1603.)

Queen Elizabeth ruled Shakespeare's mother country for over four decades (1558 to 1603). Her reign helped usher in the height of the English Renaissance. This was England's version of the pan-European artistic and cultural movement which began much in 14th century Italy and gradually spread throughout the continent.

William Shakespeare was one of a handful of dramatists to emerge during this time. While today he is revered as the foremost and most singular of all English playwrights, in his time he was merely seen as one of many theater actors and writers. His contemporaries included Christopher Marlowe, Ben Jonson, George Chapman, John Fletcher, and Thomas Dekker, among others.

The seeming proliferation of dramatists of this period was due to the fact that English theater plays were quite popular with all classes of society. In London alone, there were around five to six playhouses operating simultaneously, often offering daily shows. At that time, London had around 100,000 inhabitants – but out of that population, an astonishing 30,000 or so people would attend theater plays at least once a week, if not more.

But this meant that William Shakespeare's plays had more than enough competition.

There was pressure to provide more exciting material, yet at the same time, give theater audiences a formula they loved.

Artistic inspirations

Like many of his contemporaries, Shakepeare would often turn to adapting historical events and reusing previous playwrights' works for his stage.

Scholars theorize that Shakespeare's main inspiration was likely an earlier "Hamlet" play, which they have nicknamed "Ur-Hamlet" (from the German prefix "Ur" meaning "primordial"). It is believed to have been written in the 1580s by the English playwright Thomas Kyd, a now-less known contemporary of Shakespeare's. Unfortunately no copy of it seems to have survived; passing mentions of it in comments by theater enthusiasts of the time are the only evidence we have that it may have ever existed.

This lost earlier "Hamlet" play was itself based on an even earlier story from a 1580 anthology of tales by Francois Belleforest called "Histoires Tragiques." And that story, in turn, was derived from an ancient Scandinavian saga of a Norse prince named Amleth (a name that means "not sane"), who pretended to be mad in order to protect himself from an uncle who murdered his father, the king. Francois Belleforest took expanded on this story, and introduced Amleth as a melancholic character.

In addition, the same Norse tale of Amleth had already been written down in a 12th century account of Danish history by the monk Saxo Grammaticus (called the Gesta Danorum). A print publication of this account was also made in 1514, and may have been available as a reference for Shakespeare in the latter half of that century.

Underneath all these purported inspirations was influence of the Roman tradition of revenge plays. The English Renaissance gave the English writers of its day better access to studies and translations of ancient Greek and Roman works, which took several medieval centuries before the birth of European printing technology to disseminate. A particular boon was the 1571 English translation of all the plays of the ancient Roman playwright Seneca. Seneca's works were prime examples of Roman drama, with its affinity for gloomy and introspective heroes, ghosts, bloody violent scenes, and the horrific consequences of revenge.

In effect, with the writing of "Hamlet," Shakespeare had picked up the baton of ancient tradition and ran with it.

Elizabethan staging

The setting of Castle Elsinore in Denmark exists in real life (actually named Kronborg), but the story is fictional, taking place in 11th century Denmark, roughly around the time of the real King Canute (who reigned from 1014 to 1035).

But though the setting is medieval, in Shakespeare's time the costumes that theater companies used were almost exclusively "hand-me-downs" or items bought from used clothing sellers. Clothes were very expensive in those days, especially the luxurious ones associated with the rich and the nobility. Made-to-order clothes were a rare luxury, except for the wealthy – and made-to-order costumes for stage plays were even rarer.

So plays like "Hamlet" would have been staged with actors wearing present-day clothing – that is, Elizabethan costumes, put together out of used luxury clothes. Historical accuracy was not a priority.

In real life, it was illegal for ordinary citizens to wear luxurious clothing equal to that of the highest nobles and the ruling family, even if they could afford it. But onstage, actors could wear clothes as expensive as the ones worn by any European royalty. The first staging of Shakespeare's "Hamlet" probably had the lead actor – very likely Richard Burbage – wearing a costume fit for any European prince.

The costumes and props were also the main "special effect" in Elizabethan stage plays. Special backdrops and structures onstage were also expensive to put up, so the stage was frequently bare of ornament.

The Elizabethan audience

You might be tempted to think this sort of bare-bones staging would be "boring" compared to more modern productions of "Hamlet." But the audiences of Shakespeare's day loved costumes, and were used to listening to the spoken word for hours on end.

In late 16th century England, illiteracy and low-brow entertainment were still common. Printed books and pamphlets were just beginning to be cheaper, but not for everyone. The cheapest (or free) forms of entertainment were usually events like bear-baiting and public executions of convicted criminals and state traitors. Stage plays were the only real, cheap, educational, spoken-word alternative that people could have, regardless of which economic class they belonged to — and so they regularly filled the playhouses.

Another characteristic of Elizabethan audiences was their preoccupation with death.

Even with the relative political stability that the reign of Queen Elizabeth I had given England for four decades, death was still something that people had to deal with on a daily basis. Medicine and medical science had made little advancements since medieval times, and the plague frequently ravaged the people of England and the rest of Europe. In fact, the years 1599 to 1606 – years that encompass the time when "Hamlet" was most likely written – a deadly epidemic called the "sweating sickness" was going through London and its neighboring areas. (In 1603 alone, over 40,000 people in London died from it.)

Not surprisingly, a play like "Hamlet," with its memorable scenes and lengthy musings on death, would be an appropriate diversion and philosophical solace for its Elizabethan audience.

THEMES

Yes, "Hamlet" is Shakespeare's lengthiest play. It usually takes anywhere from four to five hours to perform. (The role of Hamlet alone has a whopping 1,530 lines – a formidable task of memorization for any lead actor.) But it's timeless script, one that continues to resonate with more modern audiences regardless of the century it's performed in, because of the universal themes contained within it.

Revenge

The first most obvious theme of the play is the cycle of revenge.

To emphasize its cyclical nature, Shakespeare has the story begin in midcycle: Hamlet's father is already murdered and we are introduced to his son, who spends most of the play contemplating what the just course of action should be. For, as the play's plot shows (and the character of Hamlet foresees), vengeance requires more blood spilled, whether intended or not. And with more blood comes more reasons for someone else to avenge that new death.

With this theme in mind, the ghost of Hamlet's father is no mere ghost out for revenge. He embodies what the culture and politics of Hamlet's country demand of the prince: that he kill King Claudius and Queen Gertrude, as just punishment for his father's murder. This is a terrible act for Hamlet. What is a just punishment according to the standards of political vengeance is also a moral offence in Hamlet's eyes – he will be murdering his own mother and uncle.

And Hamlet's famous "To be, or not to be" speech may thus be interpreted as an encapsulation of his struggle to decide whether to avenge his father's death, or to "suffer the slings and arrows of outrageous fortune." That anguish within Hamlet is the struggle between his political responsibilities and anger, versus his Christian conscience.

But as the story unfolds, the cycle of vengeance is made clear. In his quest for vengeance, Hamlet accidentally kills Polonius, and thus becomes the target of Laertes's own revenge.

The cycle of revenge also has more than one layer to it, too.

As Hamlet seeks to punish his own beloved mother as well for marrying his father's murderer, his actions also lead another woman he loves, Ophelia, to apparently kill herself. She becomes another unintended death.

Meanwhile, the kingdom of Denmark has an ongoing feud with the neighboring kingdom of Norway. Some years prior to the start of the story, when Hamlet's royal father was still alive, he battled with King Fortinbras of Norway and killed him. The slain king of Norway's son, also named Fortinbras, is also seeking revenge for his father's death by planning a war on Denmark. And because Hamlet bears the exact name of his father, it seems imminent that the feud between

Denmark and Norway will look exactly like the way it did in the previous generation.

But how does a layered cycle of revenge end? Shakespeare seemingly presents us with an equally-layered answer: it ends in bloody reparation, with the death of all parties, including that of the avenger. Hamlet dies his mother and uncle die. Laertes kills Hamlet for killing his father Polonius and driving his sister to her death; but even as he slays Hamlet, Laertes is killed by Hamlet. And the death of the royal house of Denmark becomes the ultimate reparation for the loss of Fortinbras's father and the previous defeat of Norway.

The good death

Another theme present in "Hamlet" is the so-called art of "dying well," or ars moriendi.

Unlike modern people, the Elizabethan English were obsessed with achieving a "good death". For them, a good death was one where you died courageously, fighting for what you believed in, comforted by the fact that your final deeds and thoughts had secured you salvation and eternal life in heaven. You had to stare death in the eye, so to speak, prepared and without fear.

All throughout the play, Hamlet's thoughts seem to keep going back to the inevitability death. He even literally comes to stare death in the eye when he picks up Yorick's skull. It's a foreshadowing of his death at the end of the play.

And by the play's account, Hamlet dies a good death. He does not die by accident; it is a path he chooses in order to confront Laertes and explain himself.

Like a good Christian prince, he does not plot the assassination of King Claudius as revenge for the murder of his father. Instead, the opportunity to take a life for a life presents itself to him in his last moments – he decides to stab Claudius in self-defense, so to speak, only after Claudius has successfully poisoned him, through the help of Laertes. When the dying Laertes reveals his own participation in the plot to murder Hamlet, and begs for forgiveness, Hamlet forgives him. And Hamlet himself faces imminent death without fear, giving his last commands as the prince of Denmark to his friend Horatio, and generously bequeathing the kingdom to Norway's prince.

Madness and the madness of acting

As illustrated in "Hamlet," there's a kind of madness in trying to pinpoint the difference between acting in a play, and projecting our "true selves" to other people in real life.

The company of actors that Hamlet hires are definitely only acting out their roles. But what of Claudius and Gertrude –are they not also acting out, but pretending to be an honorable royal couple, innocent of adulterous deeds or of murdering the previous King Hamlet? And what of the rest of Hamlet's court and acquaintances – are they not being false and hiding their true personas as well, to spy on Hamlet and to advance their own interests?

Hamlet is thus lost in a world of seeming. He lives in a kingdom filled with intrigue and spying. And he must navigate it while trying to find the truth behind his father's death. He cannot even trust his own mother. He cannot even trust what the ghost of his father has told him – is the ghost telling the truth? Or is the ghost merely a product of Hamlet's own troubled mind, trying to lie to himself?

Hamlet cannot even trust himself completely. It's enough to drive anyone mad. And it has, so it seems, driven Hamlet partly crazy.

But in the midst of it all, Hamlet has moments of great lucidity, where he stops pretending. He realizes that the way out of the situation is to transcend it. Lucid or half-mad, a man has a decision to make and act upon it. He can change his circumstances, or live with them; and, whichever decision he makes, he must bear the consequences without hesitation.

This madness-and-acting theme thus gives another layer of meaning to Hamlet's "to be or not to be" soliloquy. It can be interpreted as Hamlet saying that mental illness inevitably results from postponing such a decision, or from "overthinking" it. "And thus the native hue of resolution," says Hamlet, "is sicklied o'er with the pale cast of thought, and enterprises of great pitch and moment with this regard their currents turn awry..."

It also adds extra meaning to Hamlet's final words to Horatio. He bids his friend to tell his story and his "cause aright" – to make sure his true self was revealed and remembered, instead of the mad fool he had been pretending to be.

KEY SCENES & IMPORTANT QUOTES

Here are just a few of many famous quotes from key scenes in "Hamlet." These not only capture its story and themes perfectly, but have also become classic catchphrases or wise sayings of the English language.

1. "Something is rotten in the state of Denmark." - Marcellus

(From Act 1, Scene 4.) This line belongs to the Danish officer Marcellus, who utters it as he and Horatio try to follow Hamlet's chase of the ghost of his father. In one marvelously short and memorable sentence, Marcellus captures the toxic state of internal conflict and mistrust within the kingdom, within the royal court, and within the royal family itself.

2. "To thine own self be true,
   And it must follow, as the night the day,
   Thou canst not then be false to any man.
"   - Polonius

(From Act 1, Scene 3.) These lines are part of a lengthy piece of advice Polonius gives his son Laertes. The whole speech is a list of precepts that Polonius wishes his son to be guided by – some of which, ironically, Polonius proves not to follow.

3. "There are more things in Heaven and Earth, Horatio,
   Than are dreamt of in your philosophy."
- Hamlet

(From Act 1, Scene 5.) These lines are part of the conversation Hamlet has with the ghost of his father, as it demands him to swear to avenge his death. Horatio is witness to it all and says the whole event is "wondrous strange." Hamlet chides him by saying, in effect, the universe is far stranger than what man can imagine "strange" means.

4. "The lady protests too much, methinks." - Gertrude

(From Act 3, Scene 2.) This was Queen Gertrude's reaction to the portrayal of the Queen in the opening scenes of the stage play that Hamlet commissioned a company of actors to perform. It is ironic reaction, for she does not yet fully realize the play's plot deliberately mirrors what Hamlet thinks are his mother's and uncle's crimes are.

5. "To be or not to be, that is the question."
- Hamlet

(From Act 3, Scene 1) This is the opening line of the most famous passage in the play – and perhaps, in all of Shakespeare's plays. It is the start to Hamlet's famous philosophical reflection-soliloquy on the purpose of a man's life.

6. "Alas, poor Yorick. I knew him, Horatio."
- Hamlet

(From Act 5, Scene 1.) Aside from the "To be or not to be" speech, this is the other most famous moment from the play. It is a dramatic and visually arresting moment: Hamlet takes the dead jester Yorick's skull, fresh out of a dug-out grave, into his bare hands and grimly reflects how nothing is left of the lively man who loomed so large in his childhood.

SUGGESTED STUDY

Here are a few extra topics you can explore
on your own, or use for any essay or analysis
your teacher may ask you to write.

1. The secretly rebellious Ophelia

Do some research and look up the possible
meaning of the words and songs Ophelia
utters in her mad phase. (In particular, look
up the Elizabethan symbolism in the flowers
she mentions.) To modern ears, it may
sound like meaningless chatter. But
Shakespeare devotes a lot of these mad
"chatter" lines to her, and they are peppered
with symbols that had meaning to
Elizabethan audiences. Many of these words
are symbols of Ophelia's real, quite
subversive opinions about the people around

her, particularly about King Claudius and Queen Gertrude. What do you think these opinions are?

2. The Russian ban on Hamlet

From the end of World War II to 1953, the dictatorial General Secretary of the Soviet Union, Joseph Stalin, effectively "banned" Shakespeare's "Hamlet" from being performed in his state, because he reportedly did not approve of the play. Something about "Hamlet" and the ideas that the titular character speaks of made Stalin uncomfortable.

Do some historical research on Stalin and the Soviet Union of his time, and compare it to the situation of Denmark as portrayed in the play. In your opinion, what was it about

"Hamlet" that would seem subversive to Stalin?

THE TRAGEDY OF
HAMLET, PRINCE
OF DENMARK

William Shakespeare. 1604.

Dramatis Personae

Claudius, King of Denmark.

Marcellus, Officer.

Hamlet, son to the former, and nephew to the present king.

Polonius, Lord Chamberlain.

Horatio, friend to Hamlet.

Laertes, son to Polonius.

Voltemand, courtier.

Cornelius, courtier.

Rosencrantz, courtier.

Guildenstern, courtier.

Osric, courtier.

A Gentleman, courtier.

A Priest.

Marcellus, officer.

Bernardo, officer.

Francisco, a soldier

Reynaldo, servant to Polonius.

Players.

Two Clowns, gravediggers.

Fortinbras, Prince of Norway.

A Norwegian Captain.

English Ambassadors.

Gertrude, Queen of Denmark, mother to Hamlet.

Ophelia, daughter to Polonius.

Ghost of Hamlet's Father.

Lords, Ladies, Officers, Soldiers, Sailors, Messengers,

Attendants.

SCENE.- Elsinore.

Table Of Contents

ACT I. Scene I.

Elsinore. A platform before the Castle.

Enter two Sentinels-[first,] Francisco, [who paces up and down at his post; then] Bernardo, [who approaches him].

Ber. Who's there?

Fran. Nay, answer me. Stand and unfold yourself.

Ber. Long live the King!

Fran. Bernardo?

Ber. He.

Fran. You come most carefully upon your hour.

Ber. 'Tis now struck twelve. Get thee to bed, Francisco.

Fran. For this relief much thanks. 'Tis bitter cold,

And I am sick at heart.

Ber. Have you had quiet guard?

Fran. Not a mouse stirring.

Ber. Well, good night.
  If you do meet Horatio and Marcellus,
  The rivals of my watch, bid them make haste.

Enter Horatio and Marcellus.

Fran. I think I hear them. Stand, ho! Who is there?

Hor. Friends to this ground.

Mar. And liegemen to the Dane.

Fran. Give you good night.

Mar. O, farewell, honest soldier.
  Who hath reliev'd you?

Fran. Bernardo hath my place.
  Give you good night.
                    Exit.

Mar. Holla, Bernardo!

Ber. Say-

What, is Horatio there ?

Hor. A piece of him.

Ber. Welcome, Horatio. Welcome, good
Marcellus.

Mar. What, has this thing appear'd again to-
night?

Ber. I have seen nothing.

Mar. Horatio says 'tis but our fantasy,

And will not let belief take hold of him

Touching this dreaded sight, twice seen of
us.

Therefore I have entreated him along,

With us to watch the minutes of this night,

That, if again this apparition come,

He may approve our eyes and speak to it.

Hor. Tush, tush, 'twill not appear.

Ber. Sit down awhile,

And let us once again assail your ears,

That are so fortified against our story,

What we two nights have seen.

Hor. Well, sit we down,

And let us hear Bernardo speak of this.

Ber. Last night of all,

When yond same star that's westward from the pole

Had made his course t' illume that part of heaven

Where now it burns, Marcellus and myself,

The bell then beating one-

Enter Ghost.

Mar. Peace! break thee off! Look where it comes again!

Ber. In the same figure, like the King that's dead.

Mar. Thou art a scholar; speak to it, Horatio.

Ber. Looks it not like the King? Mark it, Horatio.

Hor. Most like. It harrows me with fear and wonder.

Ber. It would be spoke to.

Mar. Question it, Horatio.

Hor. What art thou that usurp'st this time of night

    Together with that fair and warlike form

    In which the majesty of buried Denmark

    Did sometimes march? By heaven I charge thee speak!

Mar. It is offended.

Ber. See, it stalks away!

Hor. Stay! Speak, speak! I charge thee speak!

                          Exit Ghost.

Mar. 'Tis gone and will not answer.

Ber. How now, Horatio? You tremble and look pale.

    Is not this something more than fantasy?

    What think you on't?

Hor. Before my God, I might not this believe

Without the sensible and true avouch

Of mine own eyes.

Mar. Is it not like the King?

Hor. As thou art to thyself.

Such was the very armour he had on

When he th' ambitious Norway combated.

So frown'd he once when, in an angry parle,

He smote the sledded Polacks on the ice.

'Tis strange.

Mar. Thus twice before, and jump at this dead hour,

With martial stalk hath he gone by our watch.

Hor. In what particular thought to work I know not;

But, in the gross and scope of my opinion,

This bodes some strange eruption to our state.

Mar. Good now, sit down, and tell me he that knows,

Why this same strict and most observant watch

So nightly toils the subject of the land,

And why such daily cast of brazen cannon

And foreign mart for implements of war;

Why such impress of shipwrights, whose sore task

Does not divide the Sunday from the week.

What might be toward, that this sweaty haste

Doth make the night joint-labourer with the day?

Who is't that can inform me?

Hor. That can I.

At least, the whisper goes so. Our last king,

Whose image even but now appear'd to us,

Was, as you know, by Fortinbras of Norway,

Thereto prick'd on by a most emulate pride,

Dar'd to the combat; in which our valiant Hamlet

(For so this side of our known world esteem'd him)

Did slay this Fortinbras; who, by a seal'd compact,

Well ratified by law and heraldry,

Did forfeit, with his life, all those his lands

Which he stood seiz'd of, to the conqueror;

Against the which a moiety competent

Was gaged by our king; which had return'd

To the inheritance of Fortinbras,

Had he been vanquisher, as, by the same cov'nant

And carriage of the article design'd,

His fell to Hamlet. Now, sir, young Fortinbras,

Of unimproved mettle hot and full,

Hath in the skirts of Norway, here and there,

Shark'd up a list of lawless resolutes,

For food and diet, to some enterprise

That hath a stomach in't; which is no other,

As it doth well appear unto our state,

But to recover of us, by strong hand

And terms compulsatory, those foresaid lands

So by his father lost; and this, I take it,

Is the main motive of our preparations,

The source of this our watch, and the chief head

Of this post-haste and romage in the land.

Ber. I think it be no other but e'en so.

Well may it sort that this portentous figure

Comes armed through our watch, so like the King

That was and is the question of these wars.

Hor. A mote it is to trouble the mind's eye.

In the most high and palmy state of Rome,

A little ere the mightiest Julius fell,

The graves stood tenantless, and the sheeted dead

Did squeak and gibber in the Roman streets;

As stars with trains of fire, and dews of
blood,
    Disasters in the sun; and the moist star
    Upon whose influence Neptune's empire
stands
    Was sick almost to doomsday with eclipse.
    And even the like precurse of fierce events,
    As harbingers preceding still the fates
    And prologue to the omen coming on,
    Have heaven and earth together
demonstrated
    Unto our climature and countrymen.

        Enter Ghost again.

    But soft! behold! Lo, where it comes again!
    I'll cross it, though it blast me.- Stay illusion!
                        Spreads his arms.
    If thou hast any sound, or use of voice,
    Speak to me.

If there be any good thing to be done,

That may to thee do ease, and, race to me,

Speak to me.

If thou art privy to thy country's fate,

Which happily foreknowing may avoid,

O, speak!

Or if thou hast uphoarded in thy life

Extorted treasure in the womb of earth

(For which, they say, you spirits oft walk in

death),

The cock crows.

Speak of it! Stay, and speak!- Stop it,

Marcellus!

Mar. Shall I strike at it with my partisan?

Hor. Do, if it will not stand.

Ber. 'Tis here!

Hor. 'Tis here!

Mar. 'Tis gone!

Exit Ghost.

We do it wrong, being so majestical,

To offer it the show of violence;

For it is as the air, invulnerable,

And our vain blows malicious mockery.

Ber. It was about to speak, when the cock
crew.

Hor. And then it started, like a guilty thing

Upon a fearful summons. I have heard

The cock, that is the trumpet to the morn,

Doth with his lofty and shrill-sounding
throat

Awake the god of day; and at his warning,

Whether in sea or fire, in earth or air,

Th' extravagant and erring spirit hies

To his confine; and of the truth herein

This present object made probation.

Mar. It faded on the crowing of the cock.

Some say that ever, 'gainst that season
comes

Wherein our Saviour's birth is celebrated,

The bird of dawning singeth all night long;

And then, they say, no spirit dare stir abroad,

The nights are wholesome, then no planets strike,

No fairy takes, nor witch hath power to charm,

So hallow'd and so gracious is the time.

Hor. So have I heard and do in part believe it.

But look, the morn, in russet mantle clad,

Walks o'er the dew of yon high eastward hill.

Break we our watch up; and by my advice

Let us impart what we have seen to-night

Unto young Hamlet; for, upon my life,

This spirit, dumb to us, will speak to him.

Do you consent we shall acquaint him with it,

As needful in our loves, fitting our duty?

Let's do't, I pray; and I this morning know

Where we shall find him most conveniently.

Exeunt.

Scene II.

Elsinore. A room of state in the Castle.

Flourish. [Enter Claudius, King of Denmark, Gertrude the Queen, Hamlet, Polonius, Laertes and his sister Ophelia, [Voltemand, Cornelius,] Lords Attendant.

King. Though yet of Hamlet our dear brother's death
    The memory be green, and that it us befitted
    To bear our hearts in grief, and our whole kingdom
    To be contracted in one brow of woe,
    Yet so far hath discretion fought with nature
    That we with wisest sorrow think on him
    Together with remembrance of ourselves.
    Therefore our sometime sister, now our queen,

Th' imperial jointress to this warlike state,

Have we, as 'twere with a defeated joy,

With an auspicious, and a dropping eye,

With mirth in funeral, and with dirge in
marriage,

In equal scale weighing delight and dole,

Taken to wife; nor have we herein barr'd

Your better wisdoms, which have freely
gone

With this affair along. For all, our thanks.

Now follows, that you know, young
Fortinbras,

Holding a weak supposal of our worth,

Or thinking by our late dear brother's death

Our state to be disjoint and out of frame,

Colleagued with this dream of his advantage,

He hath not fail'd to pester us with message

Importing the surrender of those lands

Lost by his father, with all bands of law,

To our most valiant brother. So much for
him.

Now for ourself and for this time of meeting.

Thus much the business is: we have here
writ

To Norway, uncle of young Fortinbras,

Who, impotent and bedrid, scarcely hears

Of this his nephew's purpose, to suppress

His further gait herein, in that the levies,

The lists, and full proportions are all made

Out of his subject; and we here dispatch

You, good Cornelius, and you, Voltemand,

For bearers of this greeting to old Norway,

Giving to you no further personal power

To business with the King, more than the
scope

Of these dilated articles allow

.   *[Gives a paper.]*

Farewell, and let your haste commend your
duty.

Cor., Volt. In that, and all things, will we show our duty.

King. We doubt it nothing. Heartily farewell.

Exeunt Voltemand and Cornelius.

And now, Laertes, what's the news with you?

You told us of some suit. What is't, Laertes?

You cannot speak of reason to the Dane

And lose your voice. What wouldst thou beg, Laertes,

That shall not be my offer, not thy asking?

The head is not more native to the heart,

The hand more instrumental to the mouth,

Than is the throne of Denmark to thy father.

What wouldst thou have, Laertes?

Laer. My dread lord,

Your leave and favour to return to France;

From whence though willingly I came to Denmark

To show my duty in your coronation,

Yet now I must confess, that duty done,

My thoughts and wishes bend again toward
France

And bow them to your gracious leave and
pardon.

King. Have you your father's leave? What says
Polonius?

Pol. He hath, my lord, wrung from me my
slow leave

By laboursome petition, and at last

Upon his will I seal'd my hard consent.

I do beseech you give him leave to go.

King. Take thy fair hour, Laertes. Time be
thine,

And thy best graces spend it at thy will!

But now, my cousin Hamlet, and my son-

Ham. [aside] A little more than kin, and less
than kind!

King. How is it that the clouds still hang on
you?

Ham. Not so, my lord. I am too much i' th' sun.

Queen. Good Hamlet, cast thy nighted colour off,

And let thine eye look like a friend on Denmark.

Do not for ever with thy vailed lids

Seek for thy noble father in the dust.

Thou know'st 'tis common. All that lives must die,

Passing through nature to eternity.

Ham. Ay, madam, it is common.

Queen. If it be,

Why seems it so particular with thee?

Ham. Seems, madam, Nay, it is. I know not 'seems.'

'Tis not alone my inky cloak, good mother,

Nor customary suits of solemn black,

Nor windy suspiration of forc'd breath,

No, nor the fruitful river in the eye,

Nor the dejected havior of the visage,

Together with all forms, moods, shapes of grief,

'That can denote me truly. These indeed seem,

For they are actions that a man might play;

But I have that within which passeth show-

These but the trappings and the suits of woe.

King. 'Tis sweet and commendable in your nature, Hamlet,

To give these mourning duties to your father;

But you must know, your father lost a father;

That father lost, lost his, and the survivor bound

In filial obligation for some term

To do obsequious sorrow. But to persever

In obstinate condolement is a course

Of impious stubbornness. 'Tis unmanly grief;

It shows a will most incorrect to heaven,

A heart unfortified, a mind impatient,

An understanding simple and unschool'd;

For what we know must be, and is as common

As any the most vulgar thing to sense,

Why should we in our peevish opposition

Take it to heart? Fie! 'tis a fault to heaven,

A fault against the dead, a fault to nature,

To reason most absurd, whose common theme

Is death of fathers, and who still hath cried,

From the first corse till he that died to-day,

'This must be so.' We pray you throw to earth

This unprevailing woe, and think of us

As of a father; for let the world take note

You are the most immediate to our throne,

And with no less nobility of love

Than that which dearest father bears his son

Do I impart toward you. For your intent

In going back to school in Wittenberg,

It is most retrograde to our desire;

And we beseech you, bend you to remain

Here in the cheer and comfort of our eye,

Our chiefest courtier, cousin, and our son.

Queen. Let not thy mother lose her prayers, Hamlet.

I pray thee stay with us, go not to Wittenberg.

Ham. I shall in all my best obey you, madam.

King. Why, 'tis a loving and a fair reply.

Be as ourself in Denmark. Madam, come.

This gentle and unforc'd accord of Hamlet

Sits smiling to my heart; in grace whereof,

No jocund health that Denmark drinks to-day

But the great cannon to the clouds shall tell,

And the King's rouse the heaven shall bruit again,

Respeaking earthly thunder. Come away.

Flourish. Exeunt all but Hamlet.

Ham. O that this too too solid flesh would melt,

Thaw, and resolve itself into a dew!

Or that the Everlasting had not fix'd

His canon 'gainst self-slaughter! O God! God!

How weary, stale, flat, and unprofitable

Seem to me all the uses of this world!

Fie on't! ah, fie! 'Tis an unweeded garden

That grows to seed; things rank and gross in nature

Possess it merely. That it should come to this!

But two months dead! Nay, not so much, not two.

So excellent a king, that was to this

Hyperion to a satyr; so loving to my mother

That he might not beteem the winds of heaven

Visit her face too roughly. Heaven and earth!

Must I remember? Why, she would hang on him

As if increase of appetite had grown

By what it fed on; and yet, within a month-

Let me not think on't! Frailty, thy name is woman!-

A little month, or ere those shoes were old

With which she followed my poor father's body

Like Niobe, all tears- why she, even she

(O God! a beast that wants discourse of reason

Would have mourn'd longer) married with my uncle;

My father's brother, but no more like my father

Than I to Hercules. Within a month,

Ere yet the salt of most unrighteous tears

Had left the flushing in her galled eyes,

She married. O, most wicked speed, to post

With such dexterity to incestuous sheets!

It is not, nor it cannot come to good.

But break my heart, for I must hold my

tongue!

Enter Horatio, Marcellus, and Bernardo.

Hor. Hail to your lordship!

Ham. I am glad to see you well.

Horatio!- or I do forget myself.

Hor. The same, my lord, and your poor

servant ever.

Ham. Sir, my good friend- I'll change that

name with you.

And what make you from Wittenberg,

Horatio?

Marcellus?

Mar. My good lord!

Ham. I am very glad to see you.- [To

Bernardo] Good even, sir.-

But what, in faith, make you from

Wittenberg?

  Hor. A truant disposition, good my lord.

  Ham. I would not hear your enemy say so,

    Nor shall you do my ear that violence

    To make it truster of your own report

    Against yourself. I know you are no truant.

    But what is your affair in Elsinore?

    We'll teach you to drink deep ere you depart.

  Hor. My lord, I came to see your father's

funeral.

  Ham. I prithee do not mock me, fellow

student.

    I think it was to see my mother's wedding.

  Hor. Indeed, my lord, it followed hard upon.

  Ham. Thrift, thrift, Horatio! The funeral bak'd

meats

    Did coldly furnish forth the marriage tables.

    Would I had met my dearest foe in heaven

Or ever I had seen that day, Horatio!

My father- methinks I see my father.

Hor. O, where, my lord?

Ham. In my mind's eye, Horatio.

Hor. I saw him once. He was a goodly king.

Ham. He was a man, take him for all in all.

I shall not look upon his like again.

Hor. My lord, I think I saw him yesternight.

Ham. Saw? who?

Hor. My lord, the King your father.

Ham. The King my father?

Hor. Season your admiration for a while

With an attent ear, till I may deliver

Upon the witness of these gentlemen,

This marvel to you.

Ham. For God's love let me hear!

Hor. Two nights together had these gentlemen

(Marcellus and Bernardo) on their watch

In the dead vast and middle of the night

Been thus encount'red. A figure like your father,

    Armed at point exactly, cap-a-pe,

    Appears before them and with solemn march

    Goes slow and stately by them. Thrice he walk'd

    By their oppress'd and fear-surprised eyes,

    Within his truncheon's length; whilst they distill'd

    Almost to jelly with the act of fear,

    Stand dumb and speak not to him. This to me

    In dreadful secrecy impart they did,

    And I with them the third night kept the watch;

    Where, as they had deliver'd, both in time,

    Form of the thing, each word made true and good,

    The apparition comes. I knew your father.

These hands are not more like.

Ham. But where was this?

Mar. My lord, upon the platform where we watch'd.

Ham. Did you not speak to it?

Hor. My lord, I did;

But answer made it none. Yet once methought

    It lifted up it head and did address

    Itself to motion, like as it would speak;

    But even then the morning cock crew loud,

    And at the sound it shrunk in haste away

    And vanish'd from our sight.

Ham. 'Tis very strange.

Hor. As I do live, my honour'd lord, 'tis true;

    And we did think it writ down in our duty

    To let you know of it.

Ham. Indeed, indeed, sirs. But this troubles me.

    Hold you the watch to-night?

Both [Mar. and Ber.] We do, my lord.

Ham. Arm'd, say you?

Both. Arm'd, my lord.

Ham. From top to toe?

Both. My lord, from head to foot.

Ham. Then saw you not his face?

Hor. O, yes, my lord! He wore his beaver up.

Ham. What, look'd he frowningly.

Hor. A countenance more in sorrow than in anger.

Ham. Pale or red?

Hor. Nay, very pale.

Ham. And fix'd his eyes upon you?

Hor. Most constantly.

Ham. I would I had been there.

Hor. It would have much amaz'd you.

Ham. Very like, very like. Stay'd it long?

Hor. While one with moderate haste might tell a hundred.

Both. Longer, longer.

Hor. Not when I saw't.

Ham. His beard was grizzled- no?

Hor. It was, as I have seen it in his life,

  A sable silver'd.

Ham. I will watch to-night.

  Perchance 'twill walk again.

Hor. I warr'nt it will.

Ham. If it assume my noble father's person,

  I'll speak to it, though hell itself should gape

  And bid me hold my peace. I pray you all,

  If you have hitherto conceal'd this sight,

  Let it be tenable in your silence still;

  And whatsoever else shall hap to-night,

  Give it an understanding but no tongue.

  I will requite your loves. So, fare you well.

  Upon the platform, 'twixt eleven and twelve,

  I'll visit you.

All. Our duty to your honour.

Ham. Your loves, as mine to you. Farewell.

                    Exeunt [all but Hamlet].

My father's spirit- in arms? All is not well.

I doubt some foul play. Would the night were come!

Till then sit still, my soul. Foul deeds will rise,

Though all the earth o'erwhelm them, to men's eyes.

Exit.

Scene III.

Elsinore. A room in the house of Polonius.

Enter Laertes and Ophelia.

Laer. My necessaries are embark'd. Farewell.
　And, sister, as the winds give benefit
　And convoy is assistant, do not sleep,
　But let me hear from you.
Oph. Do you doubt that?
Laer. For Hamlet, and the trifling of his
favour,
　Hold it a fashion, and a toy in blood;
　A violet in the youth of primy nature,
　Forward, not permanent- sweet, not lasting;
　The perfume and suppliance of a minute;
　No more.
Oph. No more but so?

Laer. Think it no more.

    For nature crescent does not grow alone

    In thews and bulk; but as this temple waxes,

    The inward service of the mind and soul

    Grows wide withal. Perhaps he loves you now,

    And now no soil nor cautel doth besmirch

    The virtue of his will; but you must fear,

    His greatness weigh'd, his will is not his own;

    For he himself is subject to his birth.

    He may not, as unvalued persons do,

    Carve for himself, for on his choice depends

    The safety and health of this whole state,

    And therefore must his choice be circumscrib'd

    Unto the voice and yielding of that body

    Whereof he is the head. Then if he says he loves you,

    It fits your wisdom so far to believe it

As he in his particular act and place

May give his saying deed; which is no further

Than the main voice of Denmark goes withal.

Then weigh what loss your honour may
sustain

If with too credent ear you list his songs,

Or lose your heart, or your chaste treasure
open

To his unmast'red importunity.

Fear it, Ophelia, fear it, my dear sister,

And keep you in the rear of your affection,

Out of the shot and danger of desire.

The chariest maid is prodigal enough

If she unmask her beauty to the moon.

Virtue itself scopes not calumnious strokes.

The canker galls the infants of the spring

Too oft before their buttons be disclos'd,

And in the morn and liquid dew of youth

Contagious blastments are most imminent.

Be wary then; best safety lies in fear.

Youth to itself rebels, though none else near.
Oph. I shall th' effect of this good lesson keep
    As watchman to my heart. But, good my
brother,
    Do not as some ungracious pastors do,
    Show me the steep and thorny way to
heaven,
    Whiles, like a puff'd and reckless libertine,
    Himself the primrose path of dalliance
treads
    And recks not his own rede.
  Laer. O, fear me not!

Enter Polonius.

    I stay too long. But here my father comes.
    A double blessing is a double grace;
    Occasion smiles upon a second leave.
  Pol. Yet here, Laertes? Aboard, aboard, for
shame!

The wind sits in the shoulder of your sail,

And you are stay'd for. There- my blessing
with thee!

And these few precepts in thy memory

Look thou character. Give thy thoughts no
tongue,

Nor any unproportion'd thought his act.

Be thou familiar, but by no means vulgar:

Those friends thou hast, and their adoption
tried,

Grapple them unto thy soul with hoops of
steel;

But do not dull thy palm with entertainment

Of each new-hatch'd, unfledg'd comrade.
Beware

Of entrance to a quarrel; but being in,

Bear't that th' opposed may beware of thee.

Give every man thine ear, but few thy voice;

Take each man's censure, but reserve thy
judgment.

Costly thy habit as thy purse can buy,

But not express'd in fancy; rich, not gaudy;

For the apparel oft proclaims the man,

And they in France of the best rank and
station

Are most select and generous, chief in that.

Neither a borrower nor a lender be;

For loan oft loses both itself and friend,

And borrowing dulls the edge of husbandry.

This above all- to thine own self be true,

And it must follow, as the night the day,

Thou canst not then be false to any man.

Farewell. My blessing season this in thee!

Laer. Most humbly do I take my leave, my
lord.

Pol. The time invites you. Go, your servants
tend.

Laer. Farewell, Ophelia, and remember well

What I have said to you.

Oph. 'Tis in my memory lock'd,

And you yourself shall keep the key of it.

Laer. Farewell.

Exit.

Pol. What is't, Ophelia, he hath said to you?

Oph. So please you, something touching the
Lord Hamlet.

Pol. Marry, well bethought!

'Tis told me he hath very oft of late

Given private time to you, and you yourself

Have of your audience been most free and
bounteous.

If it be so- as so 'tis put on me,

And that in way of caution- I must tell you

You do not understand yourself so clearly

As it behooves my daughter and your
honour.

What is between you? Give me up the truth.

Oph. He hath, my lord, of late made many
tenders

Of his affection to me.

Pol. Affection? Pooh! You speak like a green girl,

Unsifted in such perilous circumstance.

Do you believe his tenders, as you call them?

Oph. I do not know, my lord, what I should think,

Pol. Marry, I will teach you! Think yourself a baby

That you have ta'en these tenders for true pay,

Which are not sterling. Tender yourself more dearly,

Or (not to crack the wind of the poor phrase,

Running it thus) you'll tender me a fool.

Oph. My lord, he hath importun'd me with love

In honourable fashion.

Pol. Ay, fashion you may call it. Go to, go to!

Oph. And hath given countenance to his speech, my lord,

With almost all the holy vows of heaven.

Pol. Ay, springes to catch woodcocks! I do know,

When the blood burns, how prodigal the soul

Lends the tongue vows. These blazes, daughter,

Giving more light than heat, extinct in both

Even in their promise, as it is a-making,

You must not take for fire. From this time

Be something scanter of your maiden presence.

Set your entreatments at a higher rate

Than a command to parley. For Lord Hamlet,

Believe so much in him, that he is young,

And with a larger tether may he walk

Than may be given you. In few, Ophelia,

Do not believe his vows; for they are brokers,

Not of that dye which their investments
show,

    But mere implorators of unholy suits,

    Breathing like sanctified and pious bawds,

    The better to beguile. This is for all:

    I would not, in plain terms, from this time
forth

    Have you so slander any moment leisure

    As to give words or talk with the Lord
Hamlet.

    Look to't, I charge you. Come your ways.

  Oph. I shall obey, my lord.

                    Exeunt.

Scene IV.

Elsinore. The platform before the Castle.

Enter Hamlet, Horatio, and Marcellus.

Ham. The air bites shrewdly; it is very cold.

Hor. It is a nipping and an eager air.

Ham. What hour now?

Hor. I think it lacks of twelve.

Mar. No, it is struck.

Hor. Indeed? I heard it not. It then draws near
the season

Wherein the spirit held his wont to walk.

*A flourish of trumpets, and two pieces
go off.*

What does this mean, my lord?

Ham. The King doth wake to-night and takes
his rouse,

Keeps wassail, and the swagg'ring upspring reels,

And, as he drains his draughts of Rhenish down,

The kettledrum and trumpet thus bray out

The triumph of his pledge.

Hor. Is it a custom?

Ham. Ay, marry, is't;

But to my mind, though I am native here

And to the manner born, it is a custom

More honour'd in the breach than the observance.

This heavy-headed revel east and west

Makes us traduc'd and tax'd of other nations;

They clip us drunkards and with swinish phrase

Soil our addition; and indeed it takes

From our achievements, though perform'd at height,

The pith and marrow of our attribute.

So oft it chances in particular men

That, for some vicious mole of nature in them,

As in their birth,- wherein they are not guilty,

Since nature cannot choose his origin,-

By the o'ergrowth of some complexion,

Oft breaking down the pales and forts of reason,

Or by some habit that too much o'erleavens

The form of plausive manners, that these men

Carrying, I say, the stamp of one defect,

Being nature's livery, or fortune's star,

Their virtues else- be they as pure as grace,

As infinite as man may undergo-

Shall in the general censure take corruption

From that particular fault. The dram of e'il

Doth all the noble substance often dout To his own scandal.

Enter Ghost.

Hor. Look, my lord, it comes!

Ham. Angels and ministers of grace defend
us!

Be thou a spirit of health or goblin damn'd,

Bring with thee airs from heaven or blasts
from hell,

Be thy intents wicked or charitable,

Thou com'st in such a questionable shape

That I will speak to thee. I'll call thee Hamlet,

King, father, royal Dane. O, answer me?

Let me not burst in ignorance, but tell

Why thy canoniz'd bones, hearsed in death,

Have burst their cerements; why the
sepulchre

Wherein we saw thee quietly inurn'd,

Hath op'd his ponderous and marble jaws

To cast thee up again. What may this mean

That thou, dead corse, again in complete steel,

  Revisits thus the glimpses of the moon,

  Making night hideous, and we fools of nature

  So horridly to shake our disposition

  With thoughts beyond the reaches of our souls?

  Say, why is this? wherefore? What should we do?

Ghost beckons Hamlet.

Hor. It beckons you to go away with it,

  As if it some impartment did desire

  To you alone.

Mar. Look with what courteous action

  It waves you to a more removed ground.

  But do not go with it!

Hor. No, by no means!

Ham. It will not speak. Then will I follow it.

Hor. Do not, my lord!

Ham. Why, what should be the fear?

I do not set my life at a pin's fee;

And for my soul, what can it do to that,

Being a thing immortal as itself?

It waves me forth again. I'll follow it.

Hor. What if it tempt you toward the flood, my lord,

Or to the dreadful summit of the cliff

That beetles o'er his base into the sea,

And there assume some other, horrible form

Which might deprive your sovereignty of reason

And draw you into madness? Think of it.

The very place puts toys of desperation,

Without more motive, into every brain

That looks so many fadoms to the sea

And hears it roar beneath.

Ham. It waves me still.

Go on. I'll follow thee.

Mar. You shall not go, my lord.

Ham. Hold off your hands!

Hor. Be rul'd. You shall not go.

Ham. My fate cries out

And makes each petty artire in this body

As hardy as the Nemean lion's nerve.

[Ghost beckons.]

Still am I call'd. Unhand me, gentlemen.

By heaven, I'll make a ghost of him that lets me!-

I say, away!- Go on. I'll follow thee.

Exeunt Ghost and Hamlet.

Hor. He waxes desperate with imagination.

Mar. Let's follow. 'Tis not fit thus to obey him.

Hor. Have after. To what issue will this come?

Mar. Something is rotten in the state of Denmark.

Hor. Heaven will direct it.

Mar. Nay, let's follow him.

Exeunt.

Scene V.

Elsinore. The Castle. Another part of the fortifications.

Enter Ghost and Hamlet.

Ham. Whither wilt thou lead me? Speak! I'll go no further.

Ghost. Mark me.

Ham. I will.

Ghost. My hour is almost come,
  When I to sulph'rous and tormenting flames
  Must render up myself.

Ham. Alas, poor ghost!

Ghost. Pity me not, but lend thy serious hearing
  To what I shall unfold.

Ham. Speak. I am bound to hear.

Ghost. So art thou to revenge, when thou shalt hear.

Ham. What?

Ghost. I am thy father's spirit,

    Doom'd for a certain term to walk the night,

    And for the day confin'd to fast in fires,

    Till the foul crimes done in my days of nature

    Are burnt and purg'd away. But that I am forbid

    To tell the secrets of my prison house,

    I could a tale unfold whose lightest word

    Would harrow up thy soul, freeze thy young blood,

    Make thy two eyes, like stars, start from their spheres,

    Thy knotted and combined locks to part,

    And each particular hair to stand on end

    Like quills upon the fretful porcupine.

    But this eternal blazon must not be

To ears of flesh and blood. List, list, O, list!

If thou didst ever thy dear father love-

Ham. O God!

Ghost. Revenge his foul and most unnatural murther.

Ham. Murther?

Ghost. Murther most foul, as in the best it is;

But this most foul, strange, and unnatural.

Ham. Haste me to know't, that I, with wings as swift

As meditation or the thoughts of love,

May sweep to my revenge.

Ghost. I find thee apt;

And duller shouldst thou be than the fat weed

That rots itself in ease on Lethe wharf,

Wouldst thou not stir in this. Now, Hamlet, hear.

'Tis given out that, sleeping in my orchard,

A serpent stung me. So the whole ear of

Denmark

Is by a forged process of my death

Rankly abus'd. But know, thou noble youth,

The serpent that did sting thy father's life

Now wears his crown.

Ham. O my prophetic soul!

My uncle?

Ghost. Ay, that incestuous, that adulterate

beast,

With witchcraft of his wit, with traitorous

gifts-

O wicked wit and gifts, that have the power

So to seduce!- won to his shameful lust

The will of my most seeming-virtuous

queen.

O Hamlet, what a falling-off was there,

From me, whose love was of that dignity

That it went hand in hand even with the vow

I made to her in marriage, and to decline

Upon a wretch whose natural gifts were poor

To those of mine!

But virtue, as it never will be mov'd,

Though lewdness court it in a shape of heaven,

So lust, though to a radiant angel link'd,

Will sate itself in a celestial bed

And prey on garbage.

But soft! methinks I scent the morning air.

Brief let me be. Sleeping within my orchard,

My custom always of the afternoon,

Upon my secure hour thy uncle stole,

With juice of cursed hebona in a vial,

And in the porches of my ears did pour

The leperous distilment; whose effect

Holds such an enmity with blood of man

That swift as quicksilver it courses through

The natural gates and alleys of the body,

And with a sudden vigour it doth posset

And curd, like eager droppings into milk,
The thin and wholesome blood. So did it
mine;
And a most instant tetter bark'd about,
Most lazar-like, with vile and loathsome
crust
All my smooth body.
Thus was I, sleeping, by a brother's hand
Of life, of crown, of queen, at once
dispatch'd;
Cut off even in the blossoms of my sin,
Unhous'led, disappointed, unanel'd,
No reckoning made, but sent to my account
With all my imperfections on my head.
Ham. O, horrible! O, horrible! most horrible!
Ghost. If thou hast nature in thee, bear it not.
Let not the royal bed of Denmark be
A couch for luxury and damned incest.
But, howsoever thou pursuest this act,
Taint not thy mind, nor let thy soul contrive

Against thy mother aught. Leave her to
heaven,
    And to those thorns that in her bosom lodge
    To prick and sting her. Fare thee well at
once.
    The glowworm shows the matin to be near
    And gins to pale his uneffectual fire.
    Adieu, adieu, adieu! Remember me.
                Exit.

 Ham. O all you host of heaven! O earth! What
else?
    And shall I couple hell? Hold, hold, my heart!
    And you, my sinews, grow not instant old,
    But bear me stiffly up. Remember thee?
    Ay, thou poor ghost, while memory holds a
seat
    In this distracted globe. Remember thee?
    Yea, from the table of my memory
    I'll wipe away all trivial fond records,

All saws of books, all forms, all pressures past

That youth and observation copied there,

And thy commandment all alone shall live

Within the book and volume of my brain,

Unmix'd with baser matter. Yes, by heaven!

O most pernicious woman!

O villain, villain, smiling, damned villain!

My tables! Meet it is I set it down

That one may smile, and smile, and be a villain;

At least I am sure it may be so in Denmark.

[Writes.]

So, uncle, there you are. Now to my word:

It is 'Adieu, adieu! Remember me.'

I have sworn't.

Hor. (within) My lord, my lord!

Enter Horatio and Marcellus.

Mar. Lord Hamlet!

Hor. Heaven secure him!

Ham. So be it!

Mar. Illo, ho, ho, my lord!

Ham. Hillo, ho, ho, boy! Come, bird, come.

Mar. How is't, my noble lord?

Hor. What news, my lord?

Mar. O, wonderful!

Hor. Good my lord, tell it.

Ham. No, you will reveal it.

Hor. Not I, my lord, by heaven!

Mar. Nor I, my lord.

Ham. How say you then? Would heart of man once think it?

But you'll be secret?

Both. Ay, by heaven, my lord.

Ham. There's neer a villain dwelling in all Denmark

But he's an arrant knave.

Hor. There needs no ghost, my lord, come
from the grave

To tell us this.

Ham. Why, right! You are in the right!

And so, without more circumstance at all,

I hold it fit that we shake hands and part;

You, as your business and desires shall point
you,

For every man hath business and desire,

Such as it is; and for my own poor part,

Look you, I'll go pray.

Hor. These are but wild and whirling words,
my lord.

Ham. I am sorry they offend you, heartily;

Yes, faith, heartily.

Hor. There's no offence, my lord.

Ham. Yes, by Saint Patrick, but there is,
Horatio,

And much offence too. Touching this vision
here,

It is an honest ghost, that let me tell you.

For your desire to know what is between us,

O'ermaster't as you may. And now, good friends,

As you are friends, scholars, and soldiers,

Give me one poor request.

Hor. What is't, my lord? We will.

Ham. Never make known what you have seen to-night.

Both. My lord, we will not.

Ham. Nay, but swear't.

Hor. In faith,

My lord, not I.

Mar. Nor I, my lord- in faith.

Ham. Upon my sword.

Mar. We have sworn, my lord, already.

Ham. Indeed, upon my sword, indeed.

Ghost cries under the stage.

Ghost. Swear.

Ham. Aha boy, say'st thou so? Art thou there, truepenny?

Come on! You hear this fellow in the cellarage.

Consent to swear.

Hor. Propose the oath, my lord.

Ham. Never to speak of this that you have seen.

Swear by my sword.

Ghost. [beneath] Swear.

Ham. Hic et ubique? Then we'll shift our ground.

Come hither, gentlemen,

And lay your hands again upon my sword.

Never to speak of this that you have heard:

Swear by my sword.

Ghost. [beneath] Swear by his sword.

Ham. Well said, old mole! Canst work i' th' earth so fast?

A worthy pioner! Once more remove, good friends."

Hor. O day and night, but this is wondrous strange!

Ham. And therefore as a stranger give it welcome.

There are more things in heaven and earth, Horatio,

Than are dreamt of in your philosophy.

But come!

Here, as before, never, so help you mercy,

How strange or odd soe'er I bear myself

(As I perchance hereafter shall think meet

To put an antic disposition on),

That you, at such times seeing me, never shall,

With arms encumb'red thus, or this head-shake,

Or by pronouncing of some doubtful phrase,

As 'Well, well, we know,' or 'We could, an if
we would,'
Or 'If we list to speak,' or 'There be, an if
they might,'
Or such ambiguous giving out, to note
That you know aught of me- this is not to do,
So grace and mercy at your most need help
you,
Swear.

Ghost. [beneath] Swear.

[They swear.]

Ham. Rest, rest, perturbed spirit! So,
gentlemen,
With all my love I do commend me to you;
And what so poor a man as Hamlet is
May do t' express his love and friending to
you,
God willing, shall not lack. Let us go in
together;
And still your fingers on your lips, I pray.

The time is out of joint. O cursed spite

That ever I was born to set it right!

Nay, come, let's go together.

Exeunt.

Act II. Scene I.

Elsinore. A room in the house of Polonius.

Enter Polonius and Reynaldo.

Pol. Give him this money and these notes,
Reynaldo.

Rey. I will, my lord.

Pol. You shall do marvell's wisely, good
Reynaldo,

Before You visit him, to make inquire

Of his behaviour.

Rey. My lord, I did intend it.

Pol. Marry, well said, very well said. Look you,
sir,

Enquire me first what Danskers are in Paris;

And how, and who, what means, and where
they keep,

What company, at what expense; and finding

By this encompassment and drift of question

That they do know my son, come you more nearer

Than your particular demands will touch it.

Take you, as 'twere, some distant knowledge of him;

As thus, 'I know his father and his friends,

And in part him.' Do you mark this, Reynaldo?

Rey. Ay, very well, my lord.

Pol. 'And in part him, but,' you may say, 'not well.

But if't be he I mean, he's very wild

Addicted so and so'; and there put on him

What forgeries you please; marry, none so rank

As may dishonour him- take heed of that;

But, sir, such wanton, wild, and usual slips

As are companions noted and most known

To youth and liberty.

Rey. As gaming, my lord.

Pol. Ay, or drinking, fencing, swearing, quarrelling,

Drabbing. You may go so far.

Rey. My lord, that would dishonour him.

Pol. Faith, no, as you may season it in the charge.

You must not put another scandal on him,

That he is open to incontinency.

That's not my meaning. But breathe his faults so quaintly

That they may seem the taints of liberty,

The flash and outbreak of a fiery mind,

A savageness in unreclaimed blood,

Of general assault.

Rey. But, my good lord-

Pol. Wherefore should you do this?

Rey. Ay, my lord,

I would know that.

Pol. Marry, sir, here's my drift,

And I believe it is a fetch of warrant.

You laying these slight sullies on my son

As 'twere a thing a little soil'd i' th' working,

Mark you,

Your party in converse, him you would

sound,

Having ever seen in the prenominate crimes

The youth you breathe of guilty, be assur'd

He closes with you in this consequence:

'Good sir,' or so, or 'friend,' or 'gentleman'-

According to the phrase or the addition

Of man and country-

Rey. Very good, my lord.

Pol. And then, sir, does 'a this- 'a does- What

was I about to say? By the mass, I was about to

say something! Where did I leave?

Rey. At 'closes in the consequence,' at 'friend

or so,' and gentleman.'

Pol. At 'closes in the consequence'- Ay, marry!

He closes thus: 'I know the gentleman.

I saw him yesterday, or t'other day,

Or then, or then, with such or such; and, as you say,

There was 'a gaming; there o'ertook in's rouse;

There falling out at tennis'; or perchance,

'I saw him enter such a house of sale,'

Videlicet, a brothel, or so forth.

See you now-

Your bait of falsehood takes this carp of truth;

And thus do we of wisdom and of reach,

With windlasses and with assays of bias,

By indirections find directions out.

So, by my former lecture and advice,

Shall you my son. You have me, have you not?

Rey. My lord, I have.

Pol. God b' wi' ye, fare ye well!

Rey. Good my lord!

[Going.]

Pol. Observe his inclination in yourself.

Rey. I shall, my lord.

Pol. And let him ply his music.

Rey. Well, my lord.

Pol. Farewell!

Exit Reynaldo.

Enter Ophelia.

How now, Ophelia? What's the matter?

Oph. O my lord, my lord, I have been so
affrighted!

Pol. With what, i' th' name of God?

Oph. My lord, as I was sewing in my closet,

Lord Hamlet, with his doublet all unbrac'd,

No hat upon his head, his stockings foul'd,

Ungart'red, and down-gyved to his ankle;

Pale as his shirt, his knees knocking each
other,

And with a look so piteous in purport

As if he had been loosed out of hell

To speak of horrors- he comes before me.

Pol. Mad for thy love?

Oph. My lord, I do not know,

But truly I do fear it.

Pol. What said he?

Oph. He took me by the wrist and held me hard;

Then goes he to the length of all his arm,

And, with his other hand thus o'er his brow,

He falls to such perusal of my face

As he would draw it. Long stay'd he so.

At last, a little shaking of mine arm,

And thrice his head thus waving up and down,

He rais'd a sigh so piteous and profound

As it did seem to shatter all his bulk

And end his being. That done, he lets me go,

And with his head over his shoulder turn'd

He seem'd to find his way without his eyes,

For out o' doors he went without their help

And to the last bended their light on me.

Pol. Come, go with me. I will go seek the King.

This is the very ecstasy of love,

Whose violent property fordoes itself

And leads the will to desperate undertakings

As oft as any passion under heaven

That does afflict our natures. I am sorry.

What, have you given him any hard words of
late?

Oph. No, my good lord; but, as you did
command,

I did repel his letters and denied

His access to me.

Pol. That hath made him mad.

I am sorry that with better heed and
judgment

I had not quoted him. I fear'd he did but
trifle

And meant to wrack thee; but beshrew my jealousy!

By heaven, it is as proper to our age

To cast beyond ourselves in our opinions

As it is common for the younger sort

To lack discretion. Come, go we to the King.

This must be known; which, being kept close, might move

More grief to hide than hate to utter love.

Come.

Exeunt.

Scene II.

Elsinore. A room in the Castle.

Flourish. [Enter King and Queen, Rosencrantz and Guildenstern, cum aliis.

  King. Welcome, dear Rosencrantz and Guildenstern.
    Moreover that we much did long to see you,
    The need we have to use you did provoke
    Our hasty sending. Something have you heard
    Of Hamlet's transformation. So I call it,
    Sith nor th' exterior nor the inward man
    Resembles that it was. What it should be,
    More than his father's death, that thus hath put him
    So much from th' understanding of himself,

I cannot dream of. I entreat you both

That, being of so young days brought up with him,

And since so neighbour'd to his youth and haviour,

That you vouchsafe your rest here in our court

Some little time; so by your companies

To draw him on to pleasures, and to gather

So much as from occasion you may glean,

Whether aught to us unknown afflicts him thus

That, open'd, lies within our remedy.

Queen. Good gentlemen, he hath much talk'd of you,

And sure I am two men there are not living

To whom he more adheres. If it will please you

To show us so much gentry and good will

As to expend your time with us awhile

For the supply and profit of our hope,

Your visitation shall receive such thanks

As fits a king's remembrance.

Ros. Both your Majesties

Might, by the sovereign power you have of us,

Put your dread pleasures more into command

Than to entreaty.

Guil. But we both obey,

And here give up ourselves, in the full bent,

To lay our service freely at your feet,

To be commanded.

King. Thanks, Rosencrantz and gentle Guildenstern.

Queen. Thanks, Guildenstern and gentle Rosencrantz.

And I beseech you instantly to visit

My too much changed son.- Go, some of you,

And bring these gentlemen where Hamlet is.

Guil. Heavens make our presence and our practices

Pleasant and helpful to him!

Queen. Ay, amen!

Exeunt Rosencrantz and Guildenstern,
[with some Attendants].

Enter Polonius.

Pol. Th' ambassadors from Norway, my good lord,

Are joyfully return'd.

King. Thou still hast been the father of good news.

Pol. Have I, my lord? Assure you, my good liege,

I hold my duty as I hold my soul,

Both to my God and to my gracious king;

And I do think- or else this brain of mine

Hunts not the trail of policy so sure

As it hath us'd to do- that I have found

The very cause of Hamlet's lunacy.

King. O, speak of that! That do I long to hear.

Pol. Give first admittance to th' ambassadors.

My news shall be the fruit to that great feast.

King. Thyself do grace to them, and bring
them in.

[Exit Polonius.]

He tells me, my dear Gertrude, he hath found

The head and source of all your son's
distemper.

Queen. I doubt it is no other but the main,

His father's death and our o'erhasty
marriage.

King. Well, we shall sift him.

Enter Polonius, Voltemand, and Cornelius.

Welcome, my good friends.

Say, Voltemand, what from our brother
Norway?

Volt. Most fair return of greetings and desires.

Upon our first, he sent out to suppress

His nephew's levies; which to him appear'd

To be a preparation 'gainst the Polack,

But better look'd into, he truly found

It was against your Highness; whereat
griev'd,

That so his sickness, age, and impotence

Was falsely borne in hand, sends out arrests

On Fortinbras; which he, in brief, obeys,

Receives rebuke from Norway, and, in fine,

Makes vow before his uncle never more

To give th' assay of arms against your
Majesty.

Whereon old Norway, overcome with joy,

Gives him three thousand crowns in annual
fee

And his commission to employ those
soldiers,
  So levied as before, against the Polack;
  With an entreaty, herein further shown,
                    [Gives a paper.]
  That it might please you to give quiet pass
  Through your dominions for this enterprise,
  On such regards of safety and allowance
  As therein are set down.
 King. It likes us well;
  And at our more consider'd time we'll read,
  Answer, and think upon this business.
  Meantime we thank you for your well-took
labour.
  Go to your rest; at night we'll feast together.
  Most welcome home!
                    Exeunt Ambassadors.
 Pol. This business is well ended.
  My liege, and madam, to expostulate
  What majesty should be, what duty is,

Why day is day, night is night, and time is
time.

Were nothing but to waste night, day, and
time.

Therefore, since brevity is the soul of wit,

And tediousness the limbs and outward
flourishes,

I will be brief. Your noble son is mad.

Mad call I it; for, to define true madness,

What is't but to be nothing else but mad?

But let that go.

Queen. More matter, with less art.

Pol. Madam, I swear I use no art at all.

That he is mad, 'tis true: 'tis true 'tis pity;

And pity 'tis 'tis true. A foolish figure!

But farewell it, for I will use no art.

Mad let us grant him then. And now remains

That we find out the cause of this effect-

Or rather say, the cause of this defect,

For this effect defective comes by cause.

Thus it remains, and the remainder thus.

Perpend.

I have a daughter (have while she is mine),

Who in her duty and obedience, mark,

Hath given me this. Now gather, and

surmise.

[Reads] the letter.

'To the celestial, and my soul's idol, the most

beautified Ophelia,'-

That's an ill phrase, a vile phrase;

'beautified' is a vile phrase.

But you shall hear. Thus:

[Reads.]

'In her excellent white bosom, these, &c.'

Queen. Came this from Hamlet to her?

Pol. Good madam, stay awhile. I will be

faithful.

[Reads.]

'Doubt thou the stars are fire;

  Doubt that the sun doth move;

  Doubt truth to be a liar;

  But never doubt I love.

'O dear Ophelia, I am ill at these numbers; I

have not art to reckon my groans; but that I

love thee best, O most best, believe it. Adieu.

  'Thine evermore, most dear lady, whilst this

machine is to him, HAMLET.'

  This, in obedience, hath my daughter shown

me;

  And more above, hath his solicitings,

  As they fell out by time, by means, and place,

  All given to mine ear.

 King. But how hath she

  Receiv'd his love?

 Pol. What do you think of me?

 King. As of a man faithful and honourable.

Pol. I would fain prove so. But what might you think,

    When I had seen this hot love on the wing

    (As I perceiv'd it, I must tell you that,

    Before my daughter told me), what might you,

    Or my dear Majesty your queen here, think,

    If I had play'd the desk or table book,

    Or given my heart a winking, mute and dumb,

    Or look'd upon this love with idle sight?

    What might you think? No, I went round to work

    And my young mistress thus I did bespeak:

    'Lord Hamlet is a prince, out of thy star.

    This must not be.' And then I prescripts gave her,

    That she should lock herself from his resort,

    Admit no messengers, receive no tokens.

    Which done, she took the fruits of my advice,

And he, repulsed, a short tale to make,

Fell into a sadness, then into a fast,

Thence to a watch, thence into a weakness,

Thence to a lightness, and, by this

declension,

Into the madness wherein now he raves,

And all we mourn for.

King. Do you think 'tis this?

Queen. it may be, very like.

Pol. Hath there been such a time- I would fain

know that-

That I have Positively said ''Tis so,'

When it prov'd otherwise.?

King. Not that I know.

Pol. [points to his head and shoulder] Take

this from this, if

this

be otherwise.

If circumstances lead me, I will find

Where truth is hid, though it were hid indeed

   Within the centre.

   King. How may we try it further?

   Pol. You know sometimes he walks for hours together

   Here in the lobby.

   Queen. So he does indeed.

   Pol. At such a time I'll loose my daughter to him.

   Be you and I behind an arras then.

   Mark the encounter. If he love her not,

   And he not from his reason fall'n thereon

   Let me be no assistant for a state,

   But keep a farm and carters.

   King. We will try it.

Enter Hamlet, reading on a book.

Queen. But look where sadly the poor wretch comes reading.

Pol. Away, I do beseech you, both away

  I'll board him presently. O, give me leave.

    Exeunt King and Queen, [with Attendants].

  How does my good Lord Hamlet?

Ham. Well, God-a-mercy.

Pol. Do you know me, my lord?

Ham. Excellent well. You are a fishmonger.

Pol. Not I, my lord.

Ham. Then I would you were so honest a man.

Pol. Honest, my lord?

Ham. Ay, sir. To be honest, as this world goes, is to be one

man

  pick'd out of ten thousand.

Pol. That's very true, my lord.

Ham. For if the sun breed maggots in a dead dog, being a god kissing carrion. Have you a daughter?

Pol. I have, my lord.

Ham. Let her not walk i' th' sun. Conception is a blessing, but not as your daughter may conceive. Friend, look to't.

Pol. [aside] How say you by that? Still harping on my daughter. Yet he knew me not at first. He said I was a fishmonger. He is far gone, far gone! And truly in my youth I suff'red much extremity for love- very near this. I'll speak to him again.- What do you read, my lord?

Ham. Words, words, words.

Pol. What is the matter, my lord?

Ham. Between who?

Pol. I mean, the matter that you read, my lord.

Ham. Slanders, sir; for the satirical rogue says here that old men have grey beards; that their faces are wrinkled; their eyes purging thick amber and plum-tree gum; and that they have a plentiful lack of wit, together with most weak hams. All which, sir, though I most powerfully and potently believe, yet I hold it not honesty to have it thus set down; for you yourself, sir, should be old as I am if, like a crab, you could go backward.

Pol. [aside] Though this be madness, yet there is a method in't.-
  Will You walk out of the air, my lord?
  Ham. Into my grave?
  Pol. Indeed, that is out o' th' air. [Aside] How pregnant sometimes his replies are! a happiness that often madness hits on, Which reason and sanity could not so prosperously be delivered of.
I will leave him and suddenly contrive the means of meeting between him and my daughter. My honourable lord, I will most humbly take my leave of you.

Ham. You cannot, sir, take from me anything that I will more willingly part withal- except my life, except my life, except my life,

Enter Rosencrantz and Guildenstern.

Pol. Fare you well, my lord.

Ham. These tedious old fools!

Pol. You go to seek the Lord Hamlet. There he is.

Ros. [to Polonius] God save you, sir!

Exit [Polonius].

Guil. My honour'd lord!

Ros. My most dear lord!

Ham. My excellent good friends! How dost thou, Guildenstern?
Ah,

Rosencrantz! Good lads, how do ye both?

Ros. As the indifferent children of the earth.

Guil. Happy in that we are not over-happy. On Fortune's cap we are not the very button.

Ham. Nor the soles of her shoe?

Ros. Neither, my lord.

Ham. Then you live about her waist, or in the middle of her favours?

Guil. Faith, her privates we.

Ham. In the secret parts of Fortune? O! most true! She is a strumpet. What news ?

Ros. None, my lord, but that the world's grown honest.

Ham. Then is doomsday near! But your news is not true. Let me question more in particular. What have you, my good friends, deserved at the hands of Fortune that she sends you to prison hither?

Guil. Prison, my lord?

Ham. Denmark's a prison.

Ros. Then is the world one.

Ham. A goodly one; in which there are many confines, wards, and dungeons, Denmark being one o' th' worst.

Ros. We think not so, my lord.

Ham. Why, then 'tis none to you; for there is nothing either good or bad but thinking makes it so. To me it is a prison.

Ros. Why, then your ambition makes it one. 'Tis too narrow for your mind.

Ham. O God, I could be bounded in a nutshell and count myself a king of infinite space, were it not that I have bad dreams.

Guil. Which dreams indeed are ambition; for the very substance of the ambitious is merely the shadow of a dream.

Ham. A dream itself is but a shadow.

Ros. Truly, and I hold ambition of so airy and light a quality that it is but a shadow's shadow.

Ham. Then are our beggars bodies, and our monarchs and outstretch'd heroes the beggars' shadows. Shall we to th' court? for, by my fay, I cannot reason.

Both. We'll wait upon you.

Ham. No such matter! I will not sort you with the rest of my servants; for, to speak to you like an honest man, I am most dreadfully attended. But in the beaten way of friendship, what make you at Elsinore?

Ros. To visit you, my lord; no other occasion.

Ham. Beggar that I am, I am even poor in thanks; but I thank you; and sure, dear friends, my thanks are too dear a halfpenny. Were you not sent for? Is it your own inclining? Is it a free visitation? Come, deal justly with me. Come, come! Nay, speak.

Guil. What should we say, my lord?

Ham. Why, anything- but to th' purpose. You were sent for; and there is a kind of confession in your looks, which your modesties have not craft enough to colour. I know the good King and Queen have sent for you.

Ros. To what end, my lord?

Ham. That you must teach me. But let me conjure you by the rights of our fellowship, by the consonancy of our youth, by the obligation of our ever-preserved love, and by what more dear a better proposer could charge you withal, be even and direct with me, whether you were sent for or no.

Ros. [aside to Guildenstern] What say you?

Ham. [aside] Nay then, I have an eye of you.-If you love me, hold not off.

Guil. My lord, we were sent for.

Ham. I will tell you why. So shall my anticipation prevent your discovery, and your secrecy to the King and Queen moult no feather. I have of late- but wherefore I know not- lost all my mirth, forgone all custom of exercises; and indeed, it goes

So heavily with my disposition that this goodly frame, the earth, seems to me a sterile promontory; this most excellent canopy, the air, look you, this brave o'erhanging firmament, this majestical roof fretted with golden fire- why, it appeareth no other thing to me than a foul and pestilent congregation of vapours. What a piece of work is a man! how noble in reason! how infinite in faculties! in form and moving how express and admirable! In action how like an angel! in apprehension how like a god! The beauty of the world, the paragon of animals! And yet to me what is this quintessence of dust? Man delights not me- no, nor woman neither, though by your smiling you seem to say so.

Ros. My lord, there was no such stuff in my thoughts.

Ham. Why did you laugh then, when I said 'Man delights not me'?

Ros. To think, my lord, if you delight not in man, what Lenten entertainment the players shall receive from you. We coted them on the way, and hither are they coming to offer you service.

Ham. He that plays the king shall be welcome- his Majesty shall have tribute of me; the adventurous knight shall use his foil and target; the lover shall not sigh gratis; the humorous man shall end his part in peace; the clown shall make those laugh whose lungs are tickle o' th' sere; and the lady shall say her mind reely, or the blank verse shall halt for't. What players are they?

Ros. Even those you were wont to take such delight in, the tragedians of the city.

Ham. How chances it they travel? Their residence, both in reputation and profit, was better both ways.

Ros. I think their inhibition comes by the means of the late innovation.

Ham. Do they hold the same estimation they did when I was in the city? Are they so follow'd?

Ros. No indeed are they not.

Ham. How comes it? Do they grow rusty?

Ros. Nay, their endeavour keeps in the wonted pace; but there is, sir, an eyrie of children, little eyases, that cry out on the top of question and are most tyrannically clapp'd for't. These are now the fashion, and so berattle the common stages (so they call them) that many wearing rapiers are afraid of goosequills and dare scarce come thither.

Ham. What, are they children? Who maintains 'em? How are they escoted? Will they pursue the quality no longer than they can sing? Will they not say afterwards, if they should grow themselves to common players (as it is most like, if their means are no better), their writers do them wrong to make them exclaim against their own succession.

Ros. Faith, there has been much to do on both sides; and the nation holds it no sin to tarre them to controversy. There was, for a while, no money bid for argument unless the poet and the player went to cuffs in the question.

Ham. Is't possible?

Guil. O, there has been much throwing about of brains.

Ham. Do the boys carry it away?

Ros. Ay, that they do, my lord- Hercules and his load too.

Ham. It is not very strange; for my uncle is King of Denmark, and those that would make mows at him while my father lived give twenty, forty, fifty, a hundred ducats apiece for his picture in little. 'Sblood, there is something in this more than natural, if philosophy could find it out.

Flourish for the Players.

Guil. There are the players.

Ham. Gentlemen, you are welcome to Elsinore. Your hands, come!
Th' appurtenance of welcome is fashion and ceremony. Let me comply with you in this garb, lest my extent to the players (which I tell you must show fairly outwards) should more appear like entertainment than yours. You are welcome. But my uncle-father and aunt-mother are deceiv'd.

Guil. In what, my dear lord?

Ham. I am but mad north-north-west. When the wind is southerly I know a hawk from a handsaw.

Enter Polonius.

Pol. Well be with you, gentlemen!

Ham. Hark you, Guildenstern- and you too- at each ear a hearer!

That great baby you see there is not yet out of his swaddling clouts.

Ros. Happily he's the second time come to them; for they say an
Old man is twice a child.

Ham. I will prophesy he comes to tell me of the players. Mark it.-

You say right, sir; a Monday morning; twas so indeed.

Pol. My lord, I have news to tell you.

Ham. My lord, I have news to tell you. When Roscius was an actor in Rome-

Pol. The actors are come hither, my lord.

Ham. Buzz, buzz!

Pol. Upon my honour-

Ham. Then came each actor on his ass-

Pol. The best actors in the world, either for tragedy, comedy, history, pastoral, pastoral-comical, historical-pastoral, tragical-historical, tragical-comical-historical-pastoral; scene individable, or poem unlimited. Seneca cannot be too heavy, nor Plautus too light. For the law of writ and the liberty, these are the only men.

Ham. O Jephthah, judge of Israel, what a treasure hadst thou!

Pol. What treasure had he, my lord?

Ham. Why,

'One fair daughter, and no more,
The which he loved passing well.'

Pol. [aside] Still on my daughter.

Ham. Am I not i' th' right, old Jephthah?

Pol. If you call me Jephthah, my lord, I have a daughter that I love passing well.

Ham. Nay, that follows not.

Pol. What follows then, my lord?

Ham. Why,

'As by lot, God wot,' and then, you know,

'It came to pass, as most like it was.'

The first row of the pious chanson will show you more; for look where my abridgment comes.

Enter four or five Players.

You are welcome, masters; welcome, all.- I am glad to see
Thee well.- Welcome, good friends.- O, my old friend? Why, thy face is
valanc'd since I saw thee last. Com'st' thou to' beard me in Denmark?- What, my young

lady and mistress? By'r Lady, your ladyship is nearer to heaven than when I saw you last by the altitude of a chopine. Pray God your voice, like a piece of uncurrent gold, be not crack'd within the ring.- Masters, you are all welcome. We'll e'en to't like French falconers, fly at anything we see. We'll have a speech straight. Come, give us a taste of your quality. Come, a passionate speech.

1. Play. What speech, my good lord?

Ham. I heard thee speak me a speech once, but it was never acted; or if it was, not above once; for the play, I remember, pleas'd not the million, 'twas caviary to the general; but it was (as I receiv'd it, and others, whose judgments in such matters cried in the top of mine) an excellent play, well digested in the scenes, set down with as much modesty as cunning. I remember one said there were no sallets in the lines to make the matter savoury, nor no matter in the phrase that might indict the author of affectation; but call'd it an honest method, as wholesome as sweet, and by very much more handsome than fine. One speech in't I chiefly lov'd. 'Twas AEneas' tale to Dido, and thereabout of it especially where he speaks of Priam's slaughter. If it live in your memory, begin at this line- let me see, let me see:

'The rugged Pyrrhus, like th' Hyrcanian beast-'

'Tis not so; it begins with Pyrrhus:

'The rugged Pyrrhus, he whose sable arms,
Black as his purpose, did the night resemble

When he lay couched in the ominous
horse,
    Hath now this dread and black
complexion smear'd
    With heraldry more dismal. Head to foot
    Now is be total gules, horridly trick'd
    With blood of fathers, mothers, daughters,
sons,
    Bak'd and impasted with the parching
streets,
    That lend a tyrannous and a damned light
    To their lord's murther. Roasted in wrath
and fire,
    And thus o'ersized with coagulate gore,
    With eyes like carbuncles, the hellish
Pyrrhus
    Old grandsire Priam seeks.'

    So, proceed you.

Pol. Fore God, my lord, well spoken, with good accent and good discretion.

1. Play. 'Anon he finds him,
    Striking too short at Greeks. His antique sword,
    Rebellious to his arm, lies where it falls,
    Repugnant to command. Unequal match'd,
    Pyrrhus at Priam drives, in rage strikes wide;
    But with the whiff and wind of his fell sword
    Th' unnerved father falls. Then senseless Ilium,
    Seeming to feel this blow, with flaming top
    Stoops to his base, and with a hideous crash
    Takes prisoner Pyrrhus' ear. For lo! his sword,
    Which was declining on the milky head
    Of reverend Priam, seem'd i' th' air to stick.

So, as a painted tyrant, Pyrrhus stood,

And, like a neutral to his will and matter,

Did nothing.

But, as we often see, against some storm,

A silence in the heavens, the rack stand still,

The bold winds speechless, and the orb
below

As hush as death- anon the dreadful
thunder

Doth rend the region; so, after Pyrrhus'
pause,

Aroused vengeance sets him new awork;

And never did the Cyclops' hammers fall

On Mars's armour, forg'd for proof eterne,

With less remorse than Pyrrhus' bleeding
sword

Now falls on Priam.

Out, out, thou strumpet Fortune! All you
gods,

In general synod take away her power;

Break all the spokes and fellies from her wheel,

And bowl the round nave down the hill of heaven,

As low as to the fiends!

Pol. This is too long.

Ham. It shall to the barber's, with your beard.- Prithee say on.

He's for a jig or a tale of bawdry, or he sleeps. Say on; come to

Hecuba.

1. Play. 'But who, O who, had seen the mobled queen-'

Ham. 'The mobled queen'?

Pol. That's good! 'Mobled queen' is good.

1. Play. 'Run barefoot up and down, threat'ning the flames

    With bisson rheum; a clout upon that head

    Where late the diadem stood, and for a robe,

    About her lank and all o'erteemed loins,

    A blanket, in the alarm of fear caught up-

    Who this had seen, with tongue in venom steep'd

    'Gainst Fortune's state would treason have pronounc'd.

    But if the gods themselves did see her then,

    When she saw Pyrrhus make malicious sport

    In Mincing with his sword her husband's limbs,

    The instant burst of clamour that she made

    (Unless things mortal move them not at all)

    Would have made milch the burning eyes of heaven

And passion in the gods.'

Pol. Look, whe'r he has not turn'd his colour, and has tears in's eyes. Prithee no more!

Ham. 'Tis well. I'll have thee speak out the rest of this soon. Good my lord, will you see the players well bestow'd? Do you hear? Let them be well us'd; for they are the abstract and brief chronicles of the time. After your death you were better have a bad epitaph than their ill report while you live.

Pol. My lord, I will use them according to their desert.

Ham. God's bodykins, man, much better! Use every man after his desert, and who should scape whipping? Use them after your own honour and dignity. The less they deserve, the more merit is in your bounty. Take them in.

Pol. Come, sirs.

Ham. Follow him, friends. We'll hear a play
to-morrow.

Exeunt Polonius and Players [except the First].

Dost thou hear me, old friend? Can you play
'The Murther of

Gonzago'?

1. Play. Ay, my lord.

Ham. We'll ha't to-morrow night. You could,
for a need, study a speech of some dozen or
sixteen lines which I would set down and
insert in't, could you not?

1. Play. Ay, my lord.

Ham. Very well. Follow that lord- and look
you mock him not.

[Exit First Player.]

My good friends, I'll leave you till night. You
are welcome to Elsinore.

Ros. Good my lord!

Ham. Ay, so, God b' wi' ye!

[Exeunt Rosencrantz and Guildenstern

Now I am alone.

O what a rogue and peasant slave am I!

Is it not monstrous that this player here,

But in a fiction, in a dream of passion,

Could force his soul so to his own conceit

That, from her working, all his visage
wann'd,

Tears in his eyes, distraction in's aspect,

A broken voice, and his whole function
suiting

With forms to his conceit? And all for
nothing!

For Hecuba!

What's Hecuba to him, or he to Hecuba,

That he should weep for her? What would he
do,

Had he the motive and the cue for passion

That I have? He would drown the stage with
tears

And cleave the general ear with horrid
speech;
Make mad the guilty and appal the free,
Confound the ignorant, and amaze indeed
The very faculties of eyes and ears.
Yet I,
A dull and muddy-mettled rascal, peak
Like John-a-dreams, unpregnant of my
cause,
And can say nothing! No, not for a king,
Upon whose property and most dear life
A damn'd defeat was made. Am I a coward?
Who calls me villain? breaks my pate across?
Plucks off my beard and blows it in my face?
Tweaks me by th' nose? gives me the lie i' th'
throat
As deep as to the lungs? Who does me this,
ha?
'Swounds, I should take it! for it cannot be
But I am pigeon-liver'd and lack gall

To make oppression bitter, or ere this

I should have fatted all the region kites

With this slave's offal. Bloody bawdy villain!

Remorseless, treacherous, lecherous,

kindless villain!

O, vengeance!

Why, what an ass am I! This is most brave,

That I, the son of a dear father murther'd,

Prompted to my revenge by heaven and hell,

Must (like a whore) unpack my heart with

words

And fall a-cursing like a very drab,

A scullion!

Fie upon't! foh! About, my brain! Hum, I have

heard

That guilty creatures, sitting at a play,

Have by the very cunning of the scene

Been struck so to the soul that presently

They have proclaim'd their malefactions;

For murther, though it have no tongue, will speak

With most miraculous organ, I'll have these Players

Play something like the murther of my father

Before mine uncle. I'll observe his looks;

I'll tent him to the quick. If he but blench,

I know my course. The spirit that I have seen

May be a devil; and the devil hath power

T' assume a pleasing shape; yea, and perhaps

Out of my weakness and my melancholy,

As he is very potent with such spirits,

Abuses me to damn me. I'll have grounds

More relative than this. The play's the thing

Wherein I'll catch the conscience of the King.

Exit.

ACT III. Scene I.

Elsinore. A room in the Castle.

Enter King, Queen, Polonius, Ophelia,
Rosencrantz, Guildenstern, and Lords.

King. And can you by no drift of circumstance
    Get from him why he puts on this confusion,
    Grating so harshly all his days of quiet
    With turbulent and dangerous lunacy?
  Ros. He does confess he feels himself
distracted,
    But from what cause he will by no means
speak.
  Guil. Nor do we find him forward to be
sounded,
    But with a crafty madness keeps aloof
    When we would bring him on to some
confession

Of his true state.

Queen. Did he receive you well?

Ros. Most like a gentleman.

Guil. But with much forcing of his disposition.

Ros. Niggard of question, but of our demands
Most free in his reply.

Queen. Did you assay him
To any pastime?

Ros. Madam, it so fell out that certain players
We o'erraught on the way. Of these we told
him,
And there did seem in him a kind of joy
To hear of it. They are here about the court,
And, as I think, they have already order
This night to play before him.

Pol. 'Tis most true;
And he beseech'd me to entreat your
Majesties
To hear and see the matter.

King. With all my heart, and it doth much content me

To hear him so inclin'd.

Good gentlemen, give him a further edge

And drive his purpose on to these delights.

Ros. We shall, my lord.

Exeunt Rosencrantz and Guildenstern.

King. Sweet Gertrude, leave us too;

For we have closely sent for Hamlet hither,

That he, as 'twere by accident, may here

Affront Ophelia.

Her father and myself (lawful espials)

Will so bestow ourselves that, seeing unseen,

We may of their encounter frankly judge

And gather by him, as he is behav'd,

If't be th' affliction of his love, or no,

That thus he suffers for.

Queen. I shall obey you;

And for your part, Ophelia, I do wish

That your good beauties be the happy cause

Of Hamlet's wildness. So shall I hope your virtues

Will bring him to his wonted way again,

To both your honours.

Oph. Madam, I wish it may.

[Exit Queen.]

Pol. Ophelia, walk you here.- Gracious, so please you,

We will bestow ourselves.- [To Ophelia] Read on this book,

That show of such an exercise may colour

Your loneliness.- We are oft to blame in this,

'Tis too much prov'd, that with devotion's visage

And pious action we do sugar o'er

The Devil himself.

King. [aside] O, 'tis too true!

How smart a lash that speech doth give my conscience!

The harlot's cheek, beautied with plast'ring art,

Is not more ugly to the thing that helps it

Than is my deed to my most painted word.

O heavy burthen!

Pol. I hear him coming. Let's withdraw, my lord.

Exeunt King and Polonius].

Enter Hamlet.

Ham. To be, or not to be- that is the question:

Whether 'tis nobler in the mind to suffer

The slings and arrows of outrageous fortune

Or to take arms against a sea of troubles,

And by opposing end them. To die- to sleep-

No more; and by a sleep to say we end

The heartache, and the thousand natural shocks

That flesh is heir to. 'Tis a consummation

Devoutly to be wish'd. To die- to sleep.

To sleep- perchance to dream: ay, there's the rub!

For in that sleep of death what dreams may come

When we have shuffled off this mortal coil,

Must give us pause. There's the respect

That makes calamity of so long life.

For who would bear the whips and scorns of time,

Th' oppressor's wrong, the proud man's contumely,

The pangs of despis'd love, the law's delay,

The insolence of office, and the spurns

That patient merit of th' unworthy takes,

When he himself might his quietus make

With a bare bodkin? Who would these fardels bear,

To grunt and sweat under a weary life,

But that the dread of something after death-

The undiscover'd country, from whose
bourn
No traveller returns- puzzles the will,
And makes us rather bear those ills we have
Than fly to others that we know not of?
Thus conscience does make cowards of us
all,
And thus the native hue of resolution
Is sicklied o'er with the pale cast of thought,
And enterprises of great pith and moment
With this regard their currents turn awry
And lose the name of action.- Soft you now!
The fair Ophelia!- Nymph, in thy orisons
Be all my sins rememb'red.
Oph. Good my lord,
How does your honour for this many a day?
Ham. I humbly thank you; well, well, well.
Oph. My lord, I have remembrances of yours
That I have longed long to re-deliver.
I pray you, now receive them.

Ham. No, not I!

I never gave you aught.

Oph. My honour'd lord, you know right well you did,

And with them words of so sweet breath compos'd

As made the things more rich. Their perfume lost,

Take these again; for to the noble mind

Rich gifts wax poor when givers prove unkind.

There, my lord.

Ham. Ha, ha! Are you honest?

Oph. My lord?

Ham. Are you fair?

Oph. What means your lordship?

Ham. That if you be honest and fair, your honesty should admit no discourse to your beauty.

Oph. Could beauty, my lord, have better commerce than with honesty?

Ham. Ay, truly; for the power of beauty will sooner transform

honesty from what it is to a bawd than the force of honesty can translate beauty into his likeness. This was sometime a paradox, but now the time gives it proof. I did love you once.

Oph. Indeed, my lord, you made me believe so.

Ham. You should not have believ'd me; for virtue cannot so inoculate our old stock but we shall relish of it. I loved you not.

Oph. I was the more deceived.

Ham. Get thee to a nunnery! Why wouldst thou be a breeder of sinners? I am myself indifferent honest, but yet I could accuse me of such things that it were better my mother had not borne me.

I am very proud, revengeful, ambitious; with more offences at my beck than I have thoughts to put them in, imagination to give them shape, or time to act them in. What should such fellows as I do, crawling between earth and heaven? We are arrant knaves all; believe none of us. Go thy ways to a nunnery. Where's your father?

Oph. At home, my lord.

Ham. Let the doors be shut upon him, that he may play the fool nowhere but in's own house. Farewell.

Oph. O, help him, you sweet heavens!

Ham. If thou dost marry, I'll give thee this plague for thy dowry: be thou as chaste as ice, as pure as snow, thou shalt not escape calumny. Get thee to a nunnery. Go, farewell. Or if thou wilt needs marry, marry a fool; for wise men know well enough what monsters you make of them. To a nunnery, go; and quickly too.

Farewell.

Oph. O heavenly powers, restore him!

Ham. I have heard of your paintings too, well enough. God hath given you one face, and you make yourselves another. You jig, you amble, and you lisp; you nickname God's creatures and make your wantonness your ignorance. Go to, I'll no more on't! it hath made me mad. I say, we will have no more marriages. Those that are married already- all but one- shall live; the rest shall keep asthey are. To a nunnery, go.

Exit.

Oph. O, what a noble mind is here o'erthrown!

The courtier's, scholar's, soldier's, eye, tongue, sword,

Th' expectancy and rose of the fair state,

The glass of fashion and the mould of form,

Th' observ'd of all observers- quite, quite down!

And I, of ladies most deject and wretched,

That suck'd the honey of his music vows,

Now see that noble and most sovereign reason,

Like sweet bells jangled, out of tune and harsh;

That unmatch'd form and feature of blown youth

Blasted with ecstasy. O, woe is me

T' have seen what I have seen, see what I see!

Enter King and Polonius.

King. Love? his affections do not that way tend;

Nor what he spake, though it lack'd form a little,

Was not like madness. There's something in his soul

O'er which his melancholy sits on brood;

And I do doubt the hatch and the disclose

Will be some danger; which for to prevent,

I have in quick determination

Thus set it down: he shall with speed to England

For the demand of our neglected tribute.

Haply the seas, and countries different,

With variable objects, shall expel

This something-settled matter in his heart,

Whereon his brains still beating puts him thus

From fashion of himself. What think you on't?

Pol. It shall do well. But yet do I believe

The origin and commencement of his grief

Sprung from neglected love.- How now, Ophelia?

You need not tell us what Lord Hamlet said.

We heard it all.- My lord, do as you please;

But if you hold it fit, after the play

Let his queen mother all alone entreat him

To show his grief. Let her be round with him;

And I'll be plac'd so please you, in the ear

Of all their conference. If she find him not,

To England send him; or confine him where

Your wisdom best shall think.

King. It shall be so.

Madness in great ones must not unwatch'd go.

Exeunt.

Scene II.

Elsinore. hall in the Castle.

Enter Hamlet and three of the Players.

Ham. Speak the speech, I pray you, as I pronounc'd it to you, trippingly on the tongue. But if you mouth it, as many of our players do, I had as live the town crier spoke my lines. Nor do not saw the air too much with your hand, thus, but use all gently; for in the very torrent, tempest, and (as I may say) whirlwind of your passion, you must acquire and beget a temperance that may give it smoothness. O, it offends me to the soul to hear a robustious periwig-pated fellow tear a passion to tatters, to very rags, to split the cars of the groundlings, who (for the most part) are capable of nothing but inexplicable dumb shows and noise. I would have such a fellow whipp'd for o'erdoing

Termagant. It out-herods Herod. Pray you avoid it.

Player. I warrant your honour.

Ham. Be not too tame neither; but let your own discretion be your tutor. Suit the action to the word, the word to the action; with this special observance, that you o'erstep not the modesty of nature: for anything so overdone is from the purpose of playing, whose end, both at the first and now, was and is, to hold, as 'twere, the mirror up to nature; to show Virtue her own feature, scorn her own image, and the very age and body of the time his form and pressure. Now this overdone, or come tardy off, though it make the unskilful laugh, cannot but make the judicious grieve; the censure of the which one must in your allowance o'erweigh a whole theatre of others. O, there be players that I have seen play, and heard others praise, and that highly (not to speak it profanely), that, neither having the accent of Christians, nor the gait of Christian, pagan, nor man, have so strutted and bellowed that I have thought some of Nature's journeymen had made men, and not made them well, they imitated humanity so abominably.

Player. I hope we have reform'd that indifferently with us, sir.

Ham. O, reform it altogether! And let those that play your clowns speak no more than is set down for them. For there be of them that will themselves laugh, to set on some quantity of barren spectators to laugh too, though in the mean time some necessary question of the play be then to be considered. That's Villanous and shows a most pitiful ambition in the fool that uses it. Go make you ready.

Exeunt Players.

Enter Polonius, Rosencrantz, and Guildenstern.

How now, my lord? Will the King hear this
piece of work?

Pol. And the Queen too, and that presently.

Ham. Bid the players make haste, [Exit
Polonius.] Will you two help to hasten them?

Both. We will, my lord.

Exeunt they two.

Ham. What, ho, Horatio!

Enter Horatio.

Hor. Here, sweet lord, at your service.

Ham. Horatio, thou art e'en as just a man
  As e'er my conversation cop'd withal.

Hor. O, my dear lord!

Ham. Nay, do not think I flatter;

For what advancement may I hope from
thee,

That no revenue hast but thy good spirits

To feed and clothe thee? Why should the
poor be flatter'd?

No, let the candied tongue lick absurd pomp,

And crook the pregnant hinges of the knee

Where thrift may follow fawning. Dost thou
hear?

Since my dear soul was mistress of her
choice

And could of men distinguish, her election

Hath seal'd thee for herself. For thou hast
been

As one, in suff'ring all, that suffers nothing;

A man that Fortune's buffets and rewards

Hast ta'en with equal thanks; and blest are
those

Whose blood and judgment are so well
commingled

That they are not a pipe for Fortune's finger

To sound what stop she please. Give me that
man

That is not passion's slave, and I will wear
him

In my heart's core, ay, in my heart of heart,

As I do thee. Something too much of this I

There is a play to-night before the King.

One scene of it comes near the circumstance,

Which I have told thee, of my father's death.

I prithee, when thou seest that act afoot,

Even with the very comment of thy soul

Observe my uncle. If his occulted guilt

Do not itself unkennel in one speech,

It is a damned ghost that we have seen,

And my imaginations are as foul

As Vulcan's stithy. Give him heedful note;

For I mine eyes will rivet to his face,

And after we will both our judgments join

In censure of his seeming.

Hor. Well, my lord.

If he steal aught the whilst this play is
playing,

And scape detecting, I will pay the theft.

Sound a flourish. [Enter Trumpets and
Kettledrums. Danish march. [Enter King, Queen,
Polonius, Ophelia, Rosencrantz, Guildenstern,
and other Lords attendant, with the Guard
carrying torches.

Ham. They are coming to the play. I must be
idle.

Get you a place.

King. How fares our cousin Hamlet?

Ham. Excellent, i' faith; of the chameleon's
dish. I eat the air,promise-cramm'd. You
cannot feed capons so.

King. I have nothing with this answer, Hamlet.
These words are not mine.

Ham. No, nor mine now. [To Polonius] My lord, you play'd once i' th' university, you say?

Pol. That did I, my lord, and was accounted a good actor.

Ham. What did you enact?

Pol. I did enact Julius Caesar; I was kill'd i' th' Capitol; Brutus kill'd me.

Ham. It was a brute part of him to kill so capital a calf there. Be the players ready.

Ros. Ay, my lord. They stay upon your patience.

Queen. Come hither, my dear Hamlet, sit by me.

Ham. No, good mother. Here's metal more attractive.

Pol. [to the King] O, ho! do you mark that?

Ham. Lady, shall I lie in your lap?

[Sits down at Ophelia's feet.]

Oph. No, my lord.

Ham. I mean, my head upon your lap?

Oph. Ay, my lord.

Ham. Do you think I meant country matters?

Oph. I think nothing, my lord.

Ham. That's a fair thought to lie between maids' legs.

Oph. What is, my lord?

Ham. Nothing.

Oph. You are merry, my lord.

Ham. Who, I?

Oph. Ay, my lord.

Ham. O God, your only jig-maker! What should a man do but be merry?

For look you how cheerfully my mother looks, and my father died within 's two hours.

Oph. Nay 'tis twice two months, my lord.

Ham. So long? Nay then, let the devil wear black, for I'll have a suit of sables. O heavens! die two months ago, and not forgotten yet? Then there's hope a great man's memory may outlive his life half a year. But, by'r Lady, he must build churches then; or else shall he suffer not thinking on, with the hobby-horse, whose epitaph is 'For O, for O, the hobby-horse is forgot!'

Hautboys play. The dumb show enters.

Enter a King and a Queen very lovingly; the Queen embracing him and he her. She kneels, and makes show of protestation unto him. He takes her up, and declines his head upon her neck. He lays him down upon a bank of flowers. She, seeing him asleep, leaves him. Anon comes in a fellow, takes off his crown, kisses it, pours poison in the sleeper's ears, and leaves him. The Queen returns, finds the King dead, and makes passionate action. The Poisoner with some three or four

Mutes, comes in again, seem to condole with her. The dead body is carried away. The Poisoner wooes the Queen with gifts; she seems harsh and unwilling awhile, but in the end accepts his love.

Exeunt.

Oph. What means this, my lord?

Ham. Marry, this is miching malhecho; it means mischief.

Oph. Belike this show imports the argument of the play.

Enter Prologue.

Ham. We shall know by this fellow. The players cannot keep counsel; they'll tell all.

Oph. Will he tell us what this show meant?

Ham. Ay, or any show that you'll show him. Be not you asham'd to show, he'll not shame to tell you what it means.

Oph. You are naught, you are naught! I'll mark the play.

Pro. For us, and for our tragedy,
   Here stooping to your clemency,
   We beg your hearing patiently.
            [Exit.]

Ham. Is this a prologue, or the posy of a ring?
Oph. 'Tis brief, my lord.
Ham. As woman's love.

Enter [two Players as] King and Queen.

King. Full thirty times hath Phoebus' cart gone round

    Neptune's salt wash and Tellus' orbed
ground,
    And thirty dozen moons with borrowed
sheen
    About the world have times twelve thirties
been,
    Since love our hearts, and Hymen did our
hands,
    Unite comutual in most sacred bands.
  Queen. So many journeys may the sun and
moon
    Make us again count o'er ere love be done!
    But woe is me! you are so sick of late,
    So far from cheer and from your former
state.
    That I distrust you. Yet, though I distrust,
    Discomfort you, my lord, it nothing must;
    For women's fear and love holds quantity,
    In neither aught, or in extremity.

Now what my love is, proof hath made you know;

And as my love is siz'd, my fear is so.

Where love is great, the littlest doubts are fear;

Where little fears grow great, great love grows there.

King. Faith, I must leave thee, love, and shortly too;

My operant powers their functions leave to do.

And thou shalt live in this fair world behind,

Honour'd, belov'd, and haply one as kind

For husband shalt thou-

Queen. O, confound the rest!

Such love must needs be treason in my breast.

When second husband let me be accurst!

None wed the second but who killed the
first.

Ham. [aside] Wormwood, wormwood!

Queen. The instances that second marriage
move
Are base respects of thrift, but none of love.
A second time I kill my husband dead
When second husband kisses me in bed.
King. I do believe you think what now you
speak;
But what we do determine oft we break.
Purpose is but the slave to memory,
Of violent birth, but poor validity;
Which now, like fruit unripe, sticks on the
tree,
But fall unshaken when they mellow be.
Most necessary 'tis that we forget
To pay ourselves what to ourselves is debt.

What to ourselves in passion we propose,

The passion ending, doth the purpose lose.

The violence of either grief or joy

Their own enactures with themselves
destroy.

Where joy most revels, grief doth most
lament;

Grief joys, joy grieves, on slender accident.

This world is not for aye, nor 'tis not
strange

That even our loves should with our
fortunes change;

For 'tis a question left us yet to prove,

Whether love lead fortune, or else fortune
love.

The great man down, you mark his
favourite flies,

The poor advanc'd makes friends of
enemies;

And hitherto doth love on fortune tend,

For who not needs shall never lack a friend,

And who in want a hollow friend doth try,

Directly seasons him his enemy.

But, orderly to end where I begun,

Our wills and fates do so contrary run

That our devices still are overthrown;

Our thoughts are ours, their ends none of
our own.

So think thou wilt no second husband wed;

But die thy thoughts when thy first lord is
dead.

Queen. Nor earth to me give food, nor
heaven light,

Sport and repose lock from me day and
night,

To desperation turn my trust and hope,

An anchor's cheer in prison be my scope,

Each opposite that blanks the face of joy

Meet what I would have well, and it
destroy,

Both here and hence pursue me lasting strife,
   If, once a widow, ever I be wife!

Ham. If she should break it now!

King. 'Tis deeply sworn. Sweet, leave me here awhile.
   My spirits grow dull, and fain I would beguile
   The tedious day with sleep.
   Queen. Sleep rock thy brain,

                         [He] sleeps.

   And never come mischance between us twain!
Exit.

Ham. Madam, how like you this play?
   Queen. The lady doth protest too much, methinks.

Ham. O, but she'll keep her word.

King. Have you heard the argument? Is there no offence in't?

Ham. No, no! They do but jest, poison in jest; no offence i'

th'

world.

King. What do you call the play?

Ham. 'The Mousetrap.' Marry, how? Tropically. This play is the image of a murther done in Vienna. Gonzago is the duke's name; his wife, Baptista. You shall see anon. 'Tis a knavish piece of work; but what o' that? Your Majesty, and we that have free souls, it touches us not. Let the gall'd jade winch; our withers are unwrung.

Enter Lucianus.

This is one Lucianus, nephew to the King.

Oph. You are as good as a chorus, my lord.

Ham. I could interpret between you and your
love, if I could
See the puppets dallying.

Oph. You are keen, my lord, you are keen.

Ham. It would cost you a groaning to take off
my edge.

Oph. Still better, and worse.

Ham. So you must take your husbands.-
Begin, murtherer. Pox, leave thy damnable
faces, and begin! Come, the croaking raven
doth bellow for revenge.

Luc. Thoughts black, hands apt, drugs fit, and
time agreeing;
  Confederate season, else no creature
seeing;
  Thou mixture rank, of midnight weeds
collected,

With Hecate's ban thrice blasted, thrice
infected,
   Thy natural magic and dire property
   On wholesome life usurp immediately.

                    Pours the poison in his ears.

   Ham. He poisons him i' th' garden for's estate.
His name's Gonzago.
   The story is extant, and written in very
choice Italian. You shall see anon how the
murtherer gets the love of Gonzago's wife.
   Oph. The King rises.
   Ham. What, frighted with false fire?
   Queen. How fares my lord?
   Pol. Give o'er the play.
   King. Give me some light! Away!
   All. Lights, lights, lights!

                    Exeunt all but Hamlet and
Horatio.
   Ham.   Why, let the strucken deer go weep,

The hart ungalled play;

For some must watch, while some must sleep:

Thus runs the world away.

Would not this, sir, and a forest of feathers- if the rest of my fortunes turn Turk with me- with two Provincial roses on my

raz'd shoes, get me a fellowship in a cry of players, sir?

Hor. Half a share.

Ham.   A whole one I!

For thou dost know, O Damon dear,

This realm dismantled was

Of Jove himself; and now reigns here

A very, very- pajock.

Hor. You might have rhym'd.

Ham. O good Horatio, I'll take the ghost's word for a thousand pound! Didst perceive?

Hor. Very well, my lord.

Ham. Upon the talk of the poisoning?

Hor. I did very well note him.

Ham.   Aha! Come, some music! Come, the recorders!

For if the King like not the comedy,

Why then, belike he likes it not, perdy.

Come, some music!

Enter Rosencrantz and Guildenstern.

Guil. Good my lord, vouchsafe me a word with you.

Ham. Sir, a whole history.

Guil. The King, sir-

Ham. Ay, sir, what of him?

Guil. Is in his retirement, marvellous distemper'd.

Ham. With drink, sir?

Guil. No, my lord; rather with choler.

Ham. Your wisdom should show itself more richer to signify this to the doctor; for me to put him to his purgation would perhaps plunge him into far more choler.

Guil. Good my lord, put your discourse into some frame, and start not so wildly from my affair.

Ham. I am tame, sir; pronounce.

Guil. The Queen, your mother, in most great affliction of spirit hath sent me to you.

Ham. You are welcome.

Guil. Nay, good my lord, this courtesy is not of the right breed. If it shall please you to make me a wholesome answer, I will do your mother's commandment; if not, your pardon and my return shall be the end of my business.

Ham. Sir, I cannot.

Guil. What, my lord?

Ham. Make you a wholesome answer; my wit's diseas'd. But, sir, such answer as I can make, you shall command; or rather, as you say, my mother. Therefore no more, but to the matter! My mother, you say-

Ros. Then thus she says: your behaviour hath struck her into amazement and admiration.

Ham. O wonderful son, that can so stonish a mother! But is there no sequel at the heels of this mother's admiration? Impart.

Ros. She desires to speak with you in her closet ere you go to bed.

Ham. We shall obey, were she ten times our mother. Have you any further trade with us?

Ros. My lord, you once did love me.

Ham. And do still, by these pickers and stealers!

Ros. Good my lord, what is your cause of distemper? You do surely bar the door upon your own liberty, if you deny your grief's to your friend.

Ham. Sir, I lack advancement.

Ros. How can that be, when you have the voice of the King himself for your succession in Denmark?

Ham. Ay, sir, but 'while the grass grows'- the proverb is something musty.

Enter the Players with recorders.

O, the recorders! Let me see one. To withdraw with you- why do you go about to recover the wind of me, as if you would drive me into a toil?

Guil. O my lord, if my duty be too bold, my love is too unmannerly.

Ham. I do not well understand that. Will you play upon this pipe?

Guil. My lord, I cannot.

Ham. I pray you.

Guil. Believe me, I cannot.

Ham. I do beseech you.

Guil. I know, no touch of it, my lord.

Ham. It is as easy as lying. Govern these ventages with your fingers and thumbs, give it breath with your mouth, and it will discourse most eloquent music. Look you, these are the stops.

Guil. But these cannot I command to any utt'rance of harmony. I have not the skill.

Ham. Why, look you now, how unworthy a thing you make of me!
You would play upon me; you would seem to know my stops; you would pluck out the heart of my mystery; you would sound me from my lowest note to the top of my compass; and there is much music, excellent voice, in this little organ, yet cannot you make it speak. 'Sblood, do you think I am easier to be play'd on than

A pipe? Call me what instrument you will, though you can fret me, you cannot play upon me.

Enter Polonius.

God bless you, sir!

Pol. My lord, the Queen would speak with you, and presently.

Ham. Do you see yonder cloud that's almost in shape of a camel?

Pol. By th' mass, and 'tis like a camel indeed.

Ham. Methinks it is like a weasel.

Pol. It is back'd like a weasel.

Ham. Or like a whale.

Pol. Very like a whale.

Ham. Then will I come to my mother by-and-by.- They fool me to the top of my bent.- I will come by-and-by.

Pol. I will say so

.   *Exit.*

Ham. 'By-and-by' is easily said.- Leave me,
friends.

[Exeunt all but Hamlet.]

'Tis now the very witching time of night,

When churchyards yawn, and hell itself
breathes out

Contagion to this world. Now could I drink
hot blood

And do such bitter business as the day

Would quake to look on. Soft! now to my
mother!

O heart, lose not thy nature; let not ever

The soul of Nero enter this firm bosom.

Let me be cruel, not unnatural;

I will speak daggers to her, but use none.

My tongue and soul in this be hypocrites-

How in my words somever she be shent,

To give them seals never, my soul, consent!

Exit.

Scene III.

A room in the Castle.

Enter King, Rosencrantz, and Guildenstern.

King. I like him not, nor stands it safe with us
   To let his madness range. Therefore prepare
you;
   I your commission will forthwith dispatch,
   And he to England shall along with you.
   The terms of our estate may not endure
   Hazard so near us as doth hourly grow
   Out of his lunacies.
Guil. We will ourselves provide.
   Most holy and religious fear it is
   To keep those many many bodies safe
   That live and feed upon your Majesty.
Ros. The single and peculiar life is bound

With all the strength and armour of the mind

To keep itself from noyance; but much more

That spirit upon whose weal depends and

rests

The lives of many. The cesse of majesty

Dies not alone, but like a gulf doth draw

What's near it with it. It is a massy wheel,

Fix'd on the summit of the highest mount,

To whose huge spokes ten thousand lesser

things

Are mortis'd and adjoin'd; which when it

falls,

Each small annexment, petty consequence,

Attends the boist'rous ruin. Never alone

Did the king sigh, but with a general groan.

King. Arm you, I pray you, to this speedy

voyage;

For we will fetters put upon this fear,

Which now goes too free-footed.

Both. We will haste us.

Exeunt Gentlemen.

Enter Polonius.

Pol. My lord, he's going to his mother's closet.

Behind the arras I'll convey myself

To hear the process. I'll warrant she'll tax

him home;

And, as you said, and wisely was it said,

'Tis meet that some more audience than a

mother,

Since nature makes them partial, should

o'erhear

The speech, of vantage. Fare you well, my

liege.

I'll call upon you ere you go to bed

And tell you what I know.

King. Thanks, dear my lord.

Exit [Polonius].

O, my offence is rank, it smells to heaven;

It hath the primal eldest curse upon't,

A brother's murther! Pray can I not,

Though inclination be as sharp as will.

My stronger guilt defeats my strong intent,

And, like a man to double business bound,

I stand in pause where I shall first begin,

And both neglect. What if this cursed hand

Were thicker than itself with brother's

blood,

Is there not rain enough in the sweet

heavens

To wash it white as snow? Whereto serves

mercy

But to confront the visage of offence?

And what's in prayer but this twofold force,

To be forestalled ere we come to fall,

Or pardon'd being down? Then I'll look up;

My fault is past. But, O, what form of prayer

Can serve my turn? 'Forgive me my foul

murther'?

That cannot be; since I am still possess'd

Of those effects for which I did the murther-

My crown, mine own ambition, and my

queen.

May one be pardon'd and retain th' offence?

In the corrupted currents of this world

Offence's gilded hand may shove by justice,

And oft 'tis seen the wicked prize itself

Buys out the law; but 'tis not so above.

There is no shuffling; there the action lies

In his true nature, and we ourselves

compell'd,

Even to the teeth and forehead of our faults,

To give in evidence. What then? What rests?

Try what repentance can. What can it not?

Yet what can it when one cannot repent?

O wretched state! O bosom black as death!

O limed soul, that, struggling to be free,

Art more engag'd! Help, angels! Make assay.

Bow, stubborn knees; and heart with strings of steel,

Be soft as sinews of the new-born babe!

All may be well.

He kneels.

Enter Hamlet.

Ham. Now might I do it pat, now he is praying;

And now I'll do't. And so he goes to heaven,

And so am I reveng'd. That would be scann'd.

A villain kills my father; and for that,

I, his sole son, do this same villain send

To heaven.

Why, this is hire and salary, not revenge!

He took my father grossly, full of bread,

With all his crimes broad blown, as flush as May;

And how his audit stands, who knows save
heaven?

But in our circumstance and course of
thought,

'Tis heavy with him; and am I then reveng'd,

To take him in the purging of his soul,

When he is fit and seasoned for his passage?
No.

Up, sword, and know thou a more horrid
hent.

When he is drunk asleep; or in his rage;

Or in th' incestuous pleasure of his bed;

At gaming, swearing, or about some act

That has no relish of salvation in't-

Then trip him, that his heels may kick at
heaven,

And that his soul may be as damn'd and
black

As hell, whereto it goes. My mother stays.

This physic but prolongs thy sickly days.

Exit.

King. [rises] My words fly up, my thoughts
remain below.

Words without thoughts never to heaven go.

Exit.

Scene IV.

The Queen's closet.

Enter Queen and Polonius.

Pol. He will come straight. Look you lay home
to him.

Tell him his pranks have been too broad to
bear with,

And that your Grace hath screen'd and stood
between

Much heat and him. I'll silence me even here.

Pray you be round with him.

Ham. (within) Mother, mother, mother!

Queen. I'll warrant you; fear me not.
Withdraw; I hear him coming.

*[Polonius hides behind the
arras.]*

Enter Hamlet.

Ham. Now, mother, what's the matter?

Queen. Hamlet, thou hast thy father much offended.

Ham. Mother, you have my father much offended.

Queen. Come, come, you answer with an idle tongue.

Ham. Go, go, you question with a wicked tongue.

Queen. Why, how now, Hamlet?

Ham. What's the matter now?

Queen. Have you forgot me?

Ham. No, by the rood, not so!

You are the Queen, your husband's brother's wife,

And (would it were not so!) you are my mother.

Queen. Nay, then I'll set those to you that can speak.

Ham. Come, come, and sit you down. You shall not budge;

You go not till I set you up a glass

Where you may see the inmost part of you.

Queen. What wilt thou do? Thou wilt not murther me?

Help, help, ho!

Pol. [behind] What, ho! help, help, help!

Ham. [draws] How now? a rat? Dead for a ducat, dead!

[Makes a pass through the arras and] kills Polonius.

Pol. [behind] O, I am slain!

Queen. O me, what hast thou done?

Ham. Nay, I know not. Is it the King?

Queen. O, what a rash and bloody deed is this!

Ham. A bloody deed- almost as bad, good mother,

As kill a king, and marry with his brother.

Queen. As kill a king?

Ham. Ay, lady, it was my word.

[*Lifts up the arras and sees Polonius.*]

Thou wretched, rash, intruding fool, farewell!

I took thee for thy better. Take thy fortune.

Thou find'st to be too busy is some danger.

Leave wringing of your hands. Peace! sit you down

And let me wring your heart; for so I shall

If it be made of penetrable stuff;

If damned custom have not braz'd it so

That it is proof and bulwark against sense.

Queen. What have I done that thou dar'st wag thy tongue

In noise so rude against me?

Ham. Such an act

That blurs the grace and blush of modesty;

Calls virtue hypocrite; takes off the rose

From the fair forehead of an innocent love,

And sets a blister there; makes marriage vows

As false as dicers' oaths. O, such a deed

As from the body of contraction plucks

The very soul, and sweet religion makes

A rhapsody of words! Heaven's face doth glow;

Yea, this solidity and compound mass,

With tristful visage, as against the doom,

Is thought-sick at the act.

Queen. Ah me, what act,

That roars so loud and thunders in the index?

Ham. Look here upon th's picture, and on this,

The counterfeit presentment of two brothers.

See what a grace was seated on this brow;

Hyperion's curls; the front of Jove himself;

An eye like Mars, to threaten and command;

A station like the herald Mercury

New lighted on a heaven-kissing hill:

A combination and a form indeed

Where every god did seem to set his seal

To give the world assurance of a man.

This was your husband. Look you now what follows.

Here is your husband, like a mildew'd ear

Blasting his wholesome brother. Have you eyes?

Could you on this fair mountain leave to feed,

And batten on this moor? Ha! have you eyes

You cannot call it love; for at your age

The heyday in the blood is tame, it's humble,

And waits upon the judgment; and what judgment

Would step from this to this? Sense sure you have,

Else could you not have motion; but sure that sense

Is apoplex'd; for madness would not err,

Nor sense to ecstacy was ne'er so thrall'd

But it reserv'd some quantity of choice

To serve in such a difference. What devil was't

That thus hath cozen'd you at hoodman-blind?

Eyes without feeling, feeling without sight,

Ears without hands or eyes, smelling sans all,

Or but a sickly part of one true sense

Could not so mope.

O shame! where is thy blush? Rebellious hell,

If thou canst mutine in a matron's bones,

To flaming youth let virtue be as wax

And melt in her own fire. Proclaim no shame

When the compulsive ardour gives the charge,

Since frost itself as actively doth burn,

And reason panders will.

Queen. O Hamlet, speak no more!

Thou turn'st mine eyes into my very soul,

And there I see such black and grained spots

As will not leave their tinct.

Ham. Nay, but to live

In the rank sweat of an enseamed bed,

Stew'd in corruption, honeying and making love

Over the nasty sty!

Queen. O, speak to me no more!

These words like daggers enter in mine ears.

No more, sweet Hamlet!

Ham. A murtherer and a villain!

A slave that is not twentieth part the tithe

Of your precedent lord; a vice of kings;

A cutpurse of the empire and the rule,

That from a shelf the precious diadem stole

And put it in his pocket!

Queen. No more!

Enter the Ghost in his nightgown.

Ham. A king of shreds and patches!-
   Save me and hover o'er me with your wings,
   You heavenly guards! What would your
gracious figure?
   Queen. Alas, he's mad!
   Ham. Do you not come your tardy son to
chide,
   That, laps'd in time and passion, lets go by
   Th' important acting of your dread
command?
   O, say!
 Ghost. Do not forget. This visitation
   Is but to whet thy almost blunted purpose.
   But look, amazement on thy mother sits.
   O, step between her and her fighting soul
   Conceit in weakest bodies strongest works.

Speak to her, Hamlet.

Ham. How is it with you, lady?

Queen. Alas, how is't with you,

That you do bend your eye on vacancy,

And with th' encorporal air do hold

discourse?

Forth at your eyes your spirits wildly peep;

And, as the sleeping soldiers in th' alarm,

Your bedded hairs, like life in excrements,

Start up and stand an end. O gentle son,

Upon the heat and flame of thy distemper

Sprinkle cool patience! Whereon do you

look?

Ham. On him, on him! Look you how pale he

glares!

His form and cause conjoin'd, preaching to

stones,

Would make them capable.- Do not look

upon me,

Lest with this piteous action you convert

My stern effects. Then what I have to do

Will want true colour- tears perchance for
blood.

Queen. To whom do you speak this?

Ham. Do you see nothing there?

Queen. Nothing at all; yet all that is I see.

Ham. Nor did you nothing hear?

Queen. No, nothing but ourselves.

Ham. Why, look you there! Look how it steals
away!

My father, in his habit as he liv'd!

Look where he goes even now out at the
portal!

Exit Ghost.

Queen. This is the very coinage of your brain.

This bodiless creation ecstasy

Is very cunning in.

Ham. Ecstasy?

My pulse as yours doth temperately keep
time

And makes as healthful music. It is not madness

That I have utt'red. Bring me to the test,

And I the matter will reword; which madness

Would gambol from. Mother, for love of grace,

Lay not that flattering unction to your soul

That not your trespass but my madness speaks.

It will but skin and film the ulcerous place,

Whiles rank corruption, mining all within,

Infects unseen. Confess yourself to heaven;

Repent what's past; avoid what is to come;

And do not spread the compost on the weeds

To make them ranker. Forgive me this my virtue;

For in the fatness of these pursy times

Virtue itself of vice must pardon beg-

Yea, curb and woo for leave to do him good.

Queen. O Hamlet, thou hast cleft my heart in twain.

Ham. O, throw away the worser part of it,

And live the purer with the other half,

Good night- but go not to my uncle's bed.

Assume a virtue, if you have it not.

That monster, custom, who all sense doth eat

Of habits evil, is angel yet in this,

That to the use of actions fair and good

He likewise gives a frock or livery,

That aptly is put on. Refrain to-night,

And that shall lend a kind of easiness

To the next abstinence; the next more easy;

For use almost can change the stamp of nature,

And either [master] the devil, or throw him out

With wondrous potency. Once more, good night;

    And when you are desirous to be blest,

    I'll blessing beg of you.- For this same lord,

    I do repent; but heaven hath pleas'd it so,

    To punish me with this, and this with me,

    That I must be their scourge and minister.

    I will bestow him, and will answer well

    The death I gave him. So again, good night.

    I must be cruel, only to be kind;

    Thus bad begins, and worse remains behind.

    One word more, good lady.

  Queen. What shall I do?

  Ham. Not this, by no means, that I bid you do:

    Let the bloat King tempt you again to bed;

    Pinch wanton on your cheek; call you his mouse;

    And let him, for a pair of reechy kisses,

    Or paddling in your neck with his damn'd fingers,

Make you to ravel all this matter out,

That I essentially am not in madness,

But mad in craft. 'Twere good you let him know;

For who that's but a queen, fair, sober, wise,

Would from a paddock, from a bat, a gib

Such dear concernings hide? Who would do so?

No, in despite of sense and secrecy,

Unpeg the basket on the house's top,

Let the birds fly, and like the famous ape,

To try conclusions, in the basket creep

And break your own neck down.

Queen. Be thou assur'd, if words be made of breath,

And breath of life, I have no life to breathe

What thou hast said to me.

Ham. I must to England; you know that?

Queen. Alack,

I had forgot! 'Tis so concluded on.

Ham. There's letters seal'd; and my two
schoolfellows,
 Whom I will trust as I will adders fang'd,
 They bear the mandate; they must sweep my
way
 And marshal me to knavery. Let it work;
 For 'tis the sport to have the enginer
 Hoist with his own petar; and 't shall go hard
 But I will delve one yard below their mines
 And blow them at the moon. O, 'tis most
sweet
 When in one line two crafts directly meet.
 This man shall set me packing.
 I'll lug the guts into the neighbour room.-
 Mother, good night.- Indeed, this counsellor
 Is now most still, most secret, and most
grave,
 Who was in life a foolish peating knave.
 Come, sir, to draw toward an end with you.
 Good night, mother.

[Exit the Queen. Then] Exit Hamlet, tugging in Polonius.

ACT IV. Scene I.

Elsinore. A room in the Castle.

Enter King and Queen, with Rosencrantz and Guildenstern.

King. There's matter in these sighs. These profound heaves

You must translate; 'tis fit we understand them.

Where is your son?

Queen. Bestow this place on us a little while.

       [Exeunt Rosencrantz and Guildenstern.]

Ah, mine own lord, what have I seen to-night!

King. What, Gertrude? How does Hamlet?

Queen. Mad as the sea and wind when both contend

Which is the mightier. In his lawless fit

Behind the arras hearing something stir,

Whips out his rapier, cries 'A rat, a rat!'

And in this brainish apprehension kills

The unseen good old man.

King. O heavy deed!

It had been so with us, had we been there.

His liberty is full of threats to all-

To you yourself, to us, to every one.

Alas, how shall this bloody deed be

answer'd?

It will be laid to us, whose providence

Should have kept short, restrain'd, and out of

haunt

This mad young man. But so much was our

love

We would not understand what was most fit,

But, like the owner of a foul disease,

To keep it from divulging, let it feed

Even on the pith of life. Where is he gone?

Queen. To draw apart the body he hath kill'd;
  O'er whom his very madness, like some ore
  Among a mineral of metals base,
  Shows itself pure. He weeps for what is
done.
 King. O Gertrude, come away!
  The sun no sooner shall the mountains touch
  But we will ship him hence; and this vile
deed
  We must with all our majesty and skill
  Both countenance and excuse. Ho,
Guildenstern!

Enter Rosencrantz and Guildenstern.

  Friends both, go join you with some further
aid.
  Hamlet in madness hath Polonius slain,
  And from his mother's closet hath he dragg'd
him.

Go seek him out; speak fair, and bring the body

Into the chapel. I pray you haste in this.

Exeunt [Rosencrantz and Guildenstern].

Come, Gertrude, we'll call up our wisest friends

And let them know both what we mean to do

And what's untimely done. [So haply slander-]

Whose whisper o'er the world's diameter,

As level as the cannon to his blank,

Transports his poisoned shot- may miss our name

And hit the woundless air.- O, come away!

My soul is full of discord and dismay.

Exeunt.

Scene II.

Elsinore. A passage in the Castle.

Enter Hamlet.

Ham. Safely stow'd.

Gentlemen. (within) Hamlet! Lord Hamlet!

Ham. But soft! What noise? Who calls on
Hamlet? O, here they
come.

Enter Rosencrantz and Guildenstern.

Ros. What have you done, my lord, with the
dead body?

Ham. Compounded it with dust, whereto 'tis
kin.

Ros. Tell us where 'tis, that we may take it
thence

And bear it to the chapel.

Ham. Do not believe it.

Ros. Believe what?

Ham. That I can keep your counsel and not mine own. Besides, to be demanded of a sponge, what replication should be made by the son of a king?

Ros. Take you me for a sponge, my lord?

Ham. Ay, sir; that soaks up the King's countenance, his rewards, his authorities. But such officers do the King best service in the end. He keeps them, like an ape, in the corner of his jaw; first mouth'd, to be last swallowed. When he needs what you have

glean'd, it is but squeezing you and, sponge, you shall be dry again.

Ros. I understand you not, my lord.

Ham. I am glad of it. A knavish speech sleeps in a foolish ear.

Ros. My lord, you must tell us where the body is and go with us to the King.

Ham. The body is with the King, but the King is not with the body.

The King is a thing-

Guil. A thing, my lord?

Ham. Of nothing. Bring me to him. Hide fox, and all after.

Exeunt.

Scene III.

Elsinore. A room in the Castle.

Enter King.

King. I have sent to seek him and to find the body.

How dangerous is it that this man goes loose!

Yet must not we put the strong law on him.

He's lov'd of the distracted multitude,

Who like not in their judgment, but their eyes;

And where 'tis so, th' offender's scourge is weigh'd,

But never the offence. To bear all smooth and even,

This sudden sending him away must seem

Deliberate pause. Diseases desperate grown

By desperate appliance are reliev'd,
Or not at all.

Enter Rosencrantz.

How now O What hath befall'n?
Ros. Where the dead body is bestow'd, my
lord,
We cannot get from him.
King. But where is he?
Ros. Without, my lord; guarded, to know your
pleasure.
King. Bring him before us.
Ros. Ho, Guildenstern! Bring in my lord.

*Enter Hamlet and Guildenstern [with
Attendants].*

King. Now, Hamlet, where's Polonius?
Ham. At supper.

King. At supper? Where?

Ham. Not where he eats, but where he is eaten. A certain convocation of politic worms are e'en at him. Your worm is your only emperor for diet. We fat all creatures else to fat us, and we fat ourselves for maggots. Your fat king and your lean beggar is but variable service- two dishes, but to one table. That's the end.

King. Alas, alas!

Ham. A man may fish with the worm that hath eat of a king, and eat of the fish that hath fed of that worm.

King. What dost thou mean by this?

Ham. Nothing but to show you how a king may go a progress through the guts of a beggar.

King. Where is Polonius?

Ham. In heaven. Send thither to see. If your messenger find him not there, seek him i' th'

other place yourself. But indeed, if you find
him not within this month, you shall nose him
as you go up the stair, into the lobby.

King. Go seek him there. [To Attendants.]

Ham. He will stay till you come.

[Exeunt Attendants.]

King. Hamlet, this deed, for thine especial
safety,-

Which we do tender as we dearly grieve

For that which thou hast done,- must send
thee hence

With fiery quickness. Therefore prepare
thyself.

The bark is ready and the wind at help,

Th' associates tend, and everything is bent

For England.

Ham. For England?

King. Ay, Hamlet.

Ham. Good.

King. So is it, if thou knew'st our purposes.

Ham. I see a cherub that sees them. But come, for England!

Farewell, dear mother.

King. Thy loving father, Hamlet.

Ham. My mother! Father and mother is man and wife; man and wife is one flesh; and so, my mother. Come, for England!
Exit.

King. Follow him at foot; tempt him with speed aboard.

Delay it not; I'll have him hence to-night.

Away! for everything is seal'd and done

That else leans on th' affair. Pray you make haste.

Exeunt Rosencrantz and Guildenstern]

And, England, if my love thou hold'st at aught,-

As my great power thereof may give thee sense,

Since yet thy cicatrice looks raw and red

After the Danish sword, and thy free awe

Pays homage to us,- thou mayst not coldly
set

Our sovereign process, which imports at full,

By letters congruing to that effect,

The present death of Hamlet. Do it, England;

For like the hectic in my blood he rages,

And thou must cure me. Till I know 'tis done,

Howe'er my haps, my joys were ne'er begun.

Exit.

Scene IV.

Near Elsinore.

Enter Fortinbras with his Army over the stage.

For. Go, Captain, from me greet the Danish
king.
   Tell him that by his license Fortinbras
   Craves the conveyance of a promis'd march
   Over his kingdom. You know the
rendezvous.
   If that his Majesty would aught with us,
   We shall express our duty in his eye;
   And let him know so.
  Capt. I will do't, my lord.
  For. Go softly on.

Exeunt [all but the Captain].

Enter Hamlet, Rosencrantz, [Guildenstern,] and others.

Ham. Good sir, whose powers are these?

Capt. They are of Norway, sir.

Ham. How purpos'd, sir, I pray you?

Capt. Against some part of Poland.

Ham. Who commands them, sir?

Capt. The nephew to old Norway, Fortinbras.

Ham. Goes it against the main of Poland, sir,
  Or for some frontier?

Capt. Truly to speak, and with no addition,
  We go to gain a little patch of ground
  That hath in it no profit but the name.
  To pay five ducats, five, I would not farm it;
  Nor will it yield to Norway or the Pole
  A ranker rate, should it be sold in fee.

Ham. Why, then the Polack never will defend it.

Capt. Yes, it is already garrison'd.

Ham. Two thousand souls and twenty thousand ducats

Will not debate the question of this straw.

This is th' imposthume of much wealth and peace,

That inward breaks, and shows no cause without

Why the man dies.- I humbly thank you, sir.

Capt. God b' wi' you, sir.

[Exit.]

Ros. Will't please you go, my lord?

Ham. I'll be with you straight. Go a little before.

[Exeunt all but Hamlet.]

How all occasions do inform against me

And spur my dull revenge! What is a man,

If his chief good and market of his time

Be but to sleep and feed? A beast, no more.

Sure he that made us with such large discourse,

Looking before and after, gave us not

That capability and godlike reason

To fust in us unus'd. Now, whether it be

Bestial oblivion, or some craven scruple

Of thinking too precisely on th' event,-

A thought which, quarter'd, hath but one
part wisdom

And ever three parts coward,- I do not know

Why yet I live to say 'This thing's to do,'

Sith I have cause, and will, and strength, and
means

To do't. Examples gross as earth exhort me.

Witness this army of such mass and charge,

Led by a delicate and tender prince,

Whose spirit, with divine ambition puff'd,

Makes mouths at the invisible event,

Exposing what is mortal and unsure

To all that fortune, death, and danger dare,

Even for an eggshell. Rightly to be great

Is not to stir without great argument,

But greatly to find quarrel in a straw

When honour's at the stake. How stand I then,

That have a father kill'd, a mother stain'd,

Excitements of my reason and my blood,

And let all sleep, while to my shame I see

The imminent death of twenty thousand men

That for a fantasy and trick of fame

Go to their graves like beds, fight for a plot

Whereon the numbers cannot try the cause,

Which is not tomb enough and continent

To hide the slain? O, from this time forth,

My thoughts be bloody, or be nothing worth!

Exit.

Scene V.

Elsinore. A room in the Castle.

Enter Horatio, Queen, and a Gentleman.

Queen. I will not speak with her.

Gent. She is importunate, indeed distract.

  Her mood will needs be pitied.

Queen. What would she have?

Gent. She speaks much of her father; says she hears

  There's tricks i' th' world, and hems, and beats her heart;

  Spurns enviously at straws; speaks things in doubt,

  That carry but half sense. Her speech is nothing,

  Yet the unshaped use of it doth move

The hearers to collection; they aim at it,

And botch the words up fit to their own thoughts;

Which, as her winks and nods and gestures yield them,

Indeed would make one think there might be thought,

Though nothing sure, yet much unhappily.

Hor. 'Twere good she were spoken with; for she may strew

Dangerous conjectures in ill-breeding minds.

Queen. Let her come in.

[Exit Gentleman.]

[Aside] To my sick soul (as sin's true nature is)

Each toy seems Prologue to some great amiss.

So full of artless jealousy is guilt

It spills itself in fearing to be spilt.

Enter Ophelia distracted.

Oph. Where is the beauteous Majesty of Denmark?

Queen. How now, Ophelia?

Oph. (sings)

　　How should I your true-love know
　　　From another one?
　　By his cockle bat and' staff
　　　And his sandal shoon.

Queen. Alas, sweet lady, what imports this song?

Oph. Say you? Nay, pray You mark.

　(Sings) He is dead and gone, lady,
　　　He is dead and gone;
　　　At his head a grass-green turf,
　　　At his heels a stone.

O, ho!

Queen. Nay, but Ophelia-

Oph. Pray you mark.

(Sings) White his shroud as the mountain

snow-

Enter King.

Queen. Alas, look here, my lord!

Oph. (Sings)

    Larded all with sweet flowers;

    Which bewept to the grave did not go

    With true-love showers.

King. How do you, pretty lady?

Oph. Well, God dild you! They say the owl was

a baker's

daughter.

Lord, we know what we are, but know not what we may be. God be at
   your table!

   King. Conceit upon her father.

   Oph. Pray let's have no words of this; but when they ask, you what
   it means, say you this:

(Sings) To-morrow is Saint Valentine's day,
       All in the morning bedtime,
       And I a maid at your window,
          To be your Valentine.

       Then up he rose and donn'd his clo'es
          And dupp'd the chamber door,
       Let in the maid, that out a maid
          Never departed more.

King. Pretty Ophelia!

Oph. Indeed, la, without an oath, I'll make an end on't!

> [Sings] By Gis and by Saint Charity,
>   Alack, and fie for shame!
>   Young men will do't if they come to't
>   By Cock, they are to blame.

>   Quoth she, 'Before you tumbled me,
>   You promis'd me to wed.'

He answers:

>   'So would I 'a' done, by yonder sun,
>   An thou hadst not come to my bed.'

King. How long hath she been thus?

Oph. I hope all will be well. We must be patient; but I cannot choose but weep to think

they would lay him i' th' cold ground. My
brother shall know of it; and so I thank you for
your good counsel. Come, my coach! Good
night, ladies. Good night, sweet
 ladies. Good night, good night.

Exit

  King. Follow her close; give her good watch, I
pray you.

[Exit Horatio.]

   O, this is the poison of deep grief; it springs
   All from her father's death. O Gertrude,
Gertrude,
   When sorrows come, they come not single
spies.
   But in battalions! First, her father slain;
   Next, your son gone, and he most violent
author
   Of his own just remove; the people muddied,

Thick and and unwholesome in their
thoughts and whispers
For good Polonius' death, and we have done
but greenly
In hugger-mugger to inter him; poor Ophelia
Divided from herself and her fair judgment,
Without the which we are pictures or mere
beasts;
Last, and as much containing as all these,
Her brother is in secret come from France;
And wants not buzzers to infect his ear
Feeds on his wonder, keep, himself in clouds,
With pestilent speeches of his father's death,
Wherein necessity, of matter beggar'd,
Will nothing stick our person to arraign
In ear and ear. O my dear Gertrude, this,
Like to a murd'ring piece, in many places
Give me superfluous death.

                  A noise within.

   Queen. Alack, what noise is this?

King. Where are my Switzers? Let them guard the door.

Enter a Messenger.

What is the matter?

Mess. Save Yourself, my lord:

The ocean, overpeering of his list,

Eats not the flats with more impetuous haste

Than Young Laertes, in a riotous head,

O'erbears Your offices. The rabble call him lord;

And, as the world were now but to begin,

Antiquity forgot, custom not known,

The ratifiers and props of every word,

They cry 'Choose we! Laertes shall be king!'

Caps, hands, and tongues applaud it to the clouds,

'Laertes shall be king! Laertes king!'

                          A noise within.

Queen. How cheerfully on the false trail they cry!

O, this is counter, you false Danish dogs!

King. The doors are broke.

Enter Laertes with others.

Laer. Where is this king?- Sirs, staid you all without.

All. No, let's come in!

Laer. I pray you give me leave.

All. We will, we will!

Laer. I thank you. Keep the door.   [Exeunt his Followers.]

O thou vile king,

Give me my father!

Queen. Calmly, good Laertes.

Laer. That drop of blood that's calm proclaims me bastard;

Cries cuckold to my father; brands the harlot

Even here between the chaste unsmirched brows

Of my true mother.

King. What is the cause, Laertes,

That thy rebellion looks so giantlike?

Let him go, Gertrude. Do not fear our person.

There's such divinity doth hedge a king

That treason can but peep to what it would,

Acts little of his will. Tell me, Laertes,

Why thou art thus incens'd. Let him go, Gertrude.

Speak, man.

Laer. Where is my father?

King. Dead.

Queen. But not by him!

King. Let him demand his fill.

Laer. How came he dead? I'll not be juggled with:

To hell, allegiance! vows, to the blackest devil

Conscience and grace, to the profoundest
pit!

   I dare damnation. To this point I stand,

   That both the world, I give to negligence,

   Let come what comes; only I'll be reveng'd

   Most throughly for my father.

King. Who shall stay you?

Laer. My will, not all the world!

   And for my means, I'll husband them so well

   They shall go far with little.

King. Good Laertes,

   If you desire to know the certainty

   Of your dear father's death, is't writ in your
revenge

   That sweepstake you will draw both friend
and foe,

   Winner and loser?

Laer. None but his enemies.

King. Will you know them then?

Laer. To his good friends thus wide I'll ope my arms

And, like the kind life-rend'ring pelican,

Repast them with my blood.

King. Why, now You speak

Like a good child and a true gentleman.

That I am guiltless of your father's death,

And am most sensibly in grief for it,

It shall as level to your judgment pierce

As day does to your eye.

A noise within: 'Let her come in.'

Laer. How now? What noise is that?

Enter Ophelia.

O heat, dry up my brains! Tears seven times salt

Burn out the sense and virtue of mine eye!

By heaven, thy madness shall be paid by
weight

    Till our scale turn the beam. O rose of May!

    Dear maid, kind sister, sweet Ophelia!

    O heavens! is't possible a young maid's wits

    Should be as mortal as an old man's life?

    Nature is fine in love, and where 'tis fine,

    It sends some precious instance of itself

    After the thing it loves.

Oph. (sings)

      They bore him barefac'd on the bier

       (Hey non nony, nony, hey nony)

      And in his grave rain'd many a tear.

    Fare you well, my dove!

  Laer. Hadst thou thy wits, and didst persuade
revenge,

    It could not move thus.

Oph. You must sing 'A-down a-down, and you call him a-down-a.'
O, how the wheel becomes it! It is the false steward, that stole his master's daughter.

Laer. This nothing's more than matter.

Oph. There's rosemary, that's for remembrance. Pray you, love, remember. And there is pansies, that's for thoughts.

Laer. A document in madness! Thoughts and remembrance fitted.

Oph. There's fennel for you, and columbines. There's rue for you, and here's some for me. We may call it herb of grace o'
Sundays.

O, you must wear your rue with a difference! There's a daisy. I would give you some violets, but they wither'd all when my father died. They say he made a good end.

[Sings] For bonny sweet Robin is all my joy.

Laer. Thought and affliction, passion, hell itself,

   She turns to favour and to prettiness.

Oph. (sings)

      And will he not come again?

      And will he not come again?

       No, no, he is dead;

       Go to thy deathbed;

      He never will come again.

      His beard was as white as snow,

      All flaxen was his poll.

       He is gone, he is gone,

       And we cast away moan.

      God 'a'mercy on his soul!

   And of all Christian souls, I pray God. God b' wi' you.

Exit.

Laer. Do you see this, O God?

King. Laertes, I must commune with your grief,

Or you deny me right. Go but apart,

Make choice of whom your wisest friends you will,

And they shall hear and judge 'twixt you and me.

If by direct or by collateral hand

They find us touch'd, we will our kingdom give,

Our crown, our life, and all that we call ours,

To you in satisfaction; but if not,

Be you content to lend your patience to us,

And we shall jointly labour with your soul

To give it due content.

Laer. Let this be so.

His means of death, his obscure funeral-

No trophy, sword, nor hatchment o'er his bones,

No noble rite nor formal ostentation,-

Cry to be heard, as 'twere from heaven to earth,

That I must call't in question.

King. So you shall;

And where th' offence is let the great axe fall.

I pray you go with me.

Exeunt

Scene VI.

Elsinore. Another room in the Castle.

Enter Horatio with an Attendant.

Hor. What are they that would speak with
me?

Servant. Seafaring men, sir. They say they
have letters for you.

Hor. Let them come in.

[Exit Attendant.]

I do not know from what part of the world
I should be greeted, if not from Lord Hamlet.

Enter Sailors.

Sailor. God bless you, sir.

Hor. Let him bless thee too.

Sailor. 'A shall, sir, an't please him. There's a letter for you, sir,- it comes from th' ambassador that was bound for England- if your name be Horatio, as I am let to know it is.

Hor. (reads the letter) 'Horatio, when thou shalt have overlook'd this, give these fellows some means to the King. They have letters for him. Ere we were two days old at sea, a pirate of very warlike appointment gave us chase. Finding ourselves too slow of sail, we put on a compelled valour, and in the grapple I boarded them. On the instant they got clear of our ship; so I alone became their prisoner. They have dealt with me like thieves of mercy; but they knew what they did: I am to do a good turn for them. Let the King have the letters I have sent, and repair thou to me with as much speed as thou wouldst fly death. I have words to speak in thine ear will make thee dumb; yet are they

much too light for the bore of the matter.
These good fellows will bring thee where I am.
Rosencrantz and Guildenstern hold their
course for England. Of them I have much to tell
thee. Farewell.

       'He that thou knowest thine,
HAMLET.'

  Come, I will give you way for these your
letters,
  And do't the speedier that you may direct
me
  To him from whom you brought them.
      Exeunt.

Scene VII.

Elsinore. Another room in the Castle.

Enter King and Laertes.

  King. Now must your conscience my acquittance seal,
    And You must put me in your heart for friend,
    Sith you have heard, and with a knowing ear,
    That he which hath your noble father slain
    Pursued my life.
  Laer. It well appears. But tell me
    Why you proceeded not against these feats
    So crimeful and so capital in nature,
    As by your safety, wisdom, all things else,
    You mainly were stirr'd up.
  King. O, for two special reasons,

Which may to you, perhaps, seem much
unsinew'd,
But yet to me they are strong. The Queen his
mother
Lives almost by his looks; and for myself,-
My virtue or my plague, be it either which,-
She's so conjunctive to my life and soul
That, as the star moves not but in his sphere,
I could not but by her. The other motive
Why to a public count I might not go
Is the great love the general gender bear
him,
Who, dipping all his faults in their affection,
Would, like the spring that turneth wood to
stone,
Convert his gives to graces; so that my
arrows,
Too slightly timber'd for so loud a wind,
Would have reverted to my bow again,
And not where I had aim'd them.

Laer. And so have I a noble father lost;

  A sister driven into desp'rate terms,

  Whose worth, if praises may go back again,

  Stood challenger on mount of all the age

  For her perfections. But my revenge will
come.

 King. Break not your sleeps for that. You must
not think

  That we are made of stuff so flat and dull

  That we can let our beard be shook with
danger,

  And think it pastime. You shortly shall hear
more.

  I lov'd your father, and we love ourself,

  And that, I hope, will teach you to imagine-

     Enter a Messenger with letters.

  How now? What news?

  Mess. Letters, my lord, from Hamlet:

This to your Majesty; this to the Queen.

King. From Hamlet? Who brought them?

Mess. Sailors, my lord, they say; I saw them
not.

They were given me by Claudio; he receiv'd
them

Of him that brought them.

King. Laertes, you shall hear them.

Leave us.

Exit Messenger.

[Reads]'High and Mighty,-You shall know I
am set naked on
your

kingdom. To-morrow shall I beg leave to see
your kingly eyes;

when I shall (first asking your pardon
thereunto) recount the

occasion of my sudden and more strange
return.

'HAMLET.'

What should this mean? Are all the rest
come back?

Or is it some abuse, and no such thing?

Laer. Know you the hand?

King. 'Tis Hamlet's character. 'Naked!'

And in a postscript here, he says 'alone.'

Can you advise me?

Laer. I am lost in it, my lord. But let him come!

It warms the very sickness in my heart

That I shall live and tell him to his teeth,

'Thus didest thou.'

King. If it be so, Laertes

(As how should it be so? how otherwise?),

Will you be rul'd by me?

Laer. Ay my lord,

So you will not o'errule me to a peace.

King. To thine own peace. If he be now
return'd

As checking at his voyage, and that he means

No more to undertake it, I will work him

To exploit now ripe in my device,

Under the which he shall not choose but fall;

And for his death no wind shall breathe

But even his mother shall uncharge the

practice

And call it accident.

Laer. My lord, I will be rul'd;

The rather, if you could devise it so

That I might be the organ.

King. It falls right.

You have been talk'd of since your travel

much,

And that in Hamlet's hearing, for a quality

Wherein they say you shine, Your sum of

parts

Did not together pluck such envy from him

As did that one; and that, in my regard,

Of the unworthiest siege.

Laer. What part is that, my lord?

King. A very riband in the cap of youth-

Yet needfull too; for youth no less becomes

The light and careless livery that it wears

Than settled age his sables and his weeds,

Importing health and graveness. Two
months since

Here was a gentleman of Normandy.

I have seen myself, and serv'd against, the
French,

And they can well on horseback; but this
gallant

Had witchcraft in't. He grew unto his seat,

And to such wondrous doing brought his
horse

As had he been incorps'd and demi-natur'd

With the brave beast. So far he topp'd my
thought

That I, in forgery of shapes and tricks,

Come short of what he did.

Laer. A Norman was't?

King. A Norman.

Laer. Upon my life, Lamound.

King. The very same.

Laer. I know him well. He is the broach indeed

And gem of all the nation.

King. He made confession of you;

And gave you such a masterly report

For art and exercise in your defence,

And for your rapier most especially,

That he cried out 'twould be a sight indeed

If one could match you. The scrimers of their nation

He swore had neither motion, guard, nor eye,

If you oppos'd them. Sir, this report of his

Did Hamlet so envenom with his envy

That he could nothing do but wish and beg

Your sudden coming o'er to play with you.

Now, out of this-

Laer. What out of this, my lord?

King. Laertes, was your father dear to you?

   Or are you like the painting of a sorrow,

   A face without a heart,'

Laer. Why ask you this?

King. Not that I think you did not love your
father;

   But that I know love is begun by time,

   And that I see, in passages of proof,

   Time qualifies the spark and fire of it.

   There lives within the very flame of love

   A kind of wick or snuff that will abate it;

   And nothing is at a like goodness still;

   For goodness, growing to a plurisy,

   Dies in his own too-much. That we would do,

   We should do when we would; for this
'would' changes,

   And hath abatements and delays as many

   As there are tongues, are hands, are
accidents;

And then this 'should' is like a spendthrift sigh,

That hurts by easing. But to the quick o' th' ulcer!

Hamlet comes back. What would you undertake

To show yourself your father's son in deed

More than in words?

Laer. To cut his throat i' th' church!

King. No place indeed should murther sanctuarize;

Revenge should have no bounds. But, good Laertes,

Will you do this? Keep close within your chamber.

Hamlet return'd shall know you are come home.

We'll put on those shall praise your excellence

And set a double varnish on the fame

The Frenchman gave you; bring you in fine together

And wager on your heads. He, being remiss,

Most generous, and free from all contriving,

Will not peruse the foils; so that with ease,

Or with a little shuffling, you may choose

A sword unbated, and, in a pass of practice,

Requite him for your father.

Laer. I will do't!

And for that purpose I'll anoint my sword.

I bought an unction of a mountebank,

So mortal that, but dip a knife in it,

Where it draws blood no cataplasm so rare,

Collected from all simples that have virtue

Under the moon, can save the thing from death

This is but scratch'd withal. I'll touch my point

With this contagion, that, if I gall him slightly,

It may be death.

King. Let's further think of this,

Weigh what convenience both of time and means

May fit us to our shape. If this should fall,

And that our drift look through our bad performance.

'Twere better not assay'd. Therefore this project

Should have a back or second, that might hold

If this did blast in proof. Soft! let me see.

We'll make a solemn wager on your cunnings-

I ha't!

When in your motion you are hot and dry-

As make your bouts more violent to that end-

And that he calls for drink, I'll have prepar'd him

A chalice for the nonce; whereon but sipping,

  If he by chance escape your venom'd stuck,

  Our purpose may hold there.- But stay, what noise,

Enter Queen.

  How now, sweet queen?

  Queen. One woe doth tread upon another's heel,

  So fast they follow. Your sister's drown'd, Laertes.

  Laer. Drown'd! O, where?

  Queen. There is a willow grows aslant a brook,

  That shows his hoar leaves in the glassy stream.

  There with fantastic garlands did she come

Of crowflowers, nettles, daisies, and long
purples,
  That liberal shepherds give a grosser name,
  But our cold maids do dead men's fingers
call them.
  There on the pendant boughs her coronet
weeds
  Clamb'ring to hang, an envious sliver broke,
  When down her weedy trophies and herself
  Fell in the weeping brook. Her clothes
spread wide
  And, mermaid-like, awhile they bore her up;
  Which time she chaunted snatches of old
tunes,
  As one incapable of her own distress,
  Or like a creature native and indued
  Unto that element; but long it could not be
  Till that her garments, heavy with their
drink,

   Pull'd the poor wretch from her melodious lay

To muddy death.

  Laer. Alas, then she is drown'd?

  Queen. Drown'd, drown'd.

  Laer. Too much of water hast thou, poor Ophelia,

   And therefore I forbid my tears; but yet

   It is our trick; nature her custom holds,

   Let shame say what it will. When these are gone,

   The woman will be out. Adieu, my lord.

   I have a speech of fire, that fain would blaze

   But that this folly douts it.

                 Exit.

  King. Let's follow, Gertrude.

   How much I had to do to calm his rage I

   Now fear I this will give it start again;

   Therefore let's follow.

                 Exeunt.

ACT V. Scene I.

Elsinore. A churchyard.

Enter two Clowns, [with spades and pickaxes].

Clown. Is she to be buried in Christian burial
when she willfully seeks her own salvation?

Other. I tell thee she is; therefore make her
grave straight.

The crowner hath sate on her, and finds it
Christian burial.

Clown. How can that be, unless she drown'd
herself in her own defence?

Other. Why, 'tis found so.

Clown. It must be se offendendo; it cannot be
else. For here lies the point: if I drown myself
wittingly, it argues an act; and an act hath

three branches-it is to act, to do, and to perform; argal, she drown'd herself wittingly.

Other. Nay, but hear you, Goodman Delver!

Clown. Give me leave. Here lies the water; good. Here stands the man; good. If the man go to this water and drown himself, it is, will he nill he, he goes- mark you that. But if the water come to him and drown him, he drowns not himself. Argal, he that is not guilty of his own death shortens not his own life.

Other. But is this law?

Clown. Ay, marry, is't- crowner's quest law.

Other. Will you ha' the truth an't? If this had not been a gentlewoman, she should have been buried out o' Christian burial.

Clown. Why, there thou say'st! And the more pity that great folk should have count'nance in this world to drown or hang themselves more than their even-Christian. Come, my spade!

There is no ancient gentlemen but gard'ners, ditchers, and grave-makers.

They hold up Adam's profession.

Other. Was he a gentleman?

Clown. 'A was the first that ever bore arms.

Other. Why, he had none.

Clown. What, art a heathen? How dost thou understand the

Scripture?

The Scripture says Adam digg'd. Could he dig without arms? I'll put another question to thee. If thou answerest me not to the purpose, confess thyself-

Other. Go to!

Clown. What is he that builds stronger than either the mason, the shipwright, or the carpenter?

Other. The gallows-maker; for that frame outlives a thousand tenants.

Clown. I like thy wit well, in good faith. The
gallows does well.

But how does it well? It does well to those
that do ill. Now, thou dost ill to say the gallows
is built stronger than the church. Argal, the
gallows may do well to thee. To't again, come!

Other. Who builds stronger than a mason, a
shipwright, or a carpenter?

Clown. Ay, tell me that, and unyoke.

Other. Marry, now I can tell!

Clown. To't.

Other. Mass, I cannot tell.

Enter Hamlet and Horatio afar off.

Clown. Cudgel thy brains no more about it, for
your dull ass will not mend his pace with
beating; and when you are ask'd this question
next, say 'a grave-maker.' The houses he

makes lasts till doomsday. Go, get thee to Yaughan; fetch me a stoup of liquor.

[Exit Second Clown.]

[Clown digs and] sings.

In youth when I did love, did love,
  Methought it was very sweet;
  To contract- O- the time for- a- my behove,
    O, methought there- a- was nothing- a-
meet.

  Ham. Has this fellow no feeling of his business, that he sings at grave-making?
  Hor. Custom hath made it in him a property of easiness.
  Ham. 'Tis e'en so. The hand of little employment hath the daintier sense.
  Clown. (sings)

But age with his stealing steps

   Hath clawed me in his clutch,

And hath shipped me intil the land,

   As if I had never been such.

[Throws up a skull.]

Ham. That skull had a tongue in it, and could sing once. How the knave jowls it to the ground,as if 'twere Cain's jawbone, that did the first murther! This might be the pate of a Politician, which this ass now o'erreaches; one that would circumvent

God, might it not?

  Hor. It might, my lord.

  Ham. Or of a courtier, which could say 'Good morrow, sweet lord!

   How dost thou, good lord?' This might be my Lord Such-a-one, that prais'd my Lord Such-a-one's horse when he meant to beg it-might it not?

Hor. Ay, my lord.

Ham. Why, e'en so! and now my Lady
Worm's, chapless, and

knock'd about the mazzard with a sexton's
spade. Here's fine revolution, and we had the
trick to see't. Did these bones cost no more the
breeding but to play at loggets with 'em? Mine
ache to think

   on't.

Clown. (Sings)

   A pickaxe and a spade, a spade,

      For and a shrouding sheet;

   O, a Pit of clay for to be made

      For such a guest is meet.

                     Throws up [another skull].

Ham. There's another. Why may not that be
the skull of a lawyer? Where be his quiddits
now, his quillets, his cases, his tenures, and his
tricks? Why does he suffer this rude knave

now to knock him about the sconce with a dirty shovel, and will not tell him of his action of battery? Hum! This fellow might be in's time A great buyer of land, with his statutes, his recognizances, his fines, his double vouchers, his recoveries. Is this the fine of his fines, and the recovery of his recoveries, to have his fine pate full of fine dirt? Will his vouchers vouch him no more of his purchases, and double ones too, than the length and breadth of a pair of indentures? The very conveyances of his lands will scarcely lie in this box; and must th' inheritor himself have no more, ha?

Hor. Not a jot more, my lord.

Ham. Is not parchment made of sheepskins?

Hor. Ay, my lord, And of calveskins too.

Ham. They are sheep and calves which seek out assurance in that. I will speak to this fellow. Whose grave's this, sirrah?

Clown. Mine, sir.

[Sings] O, a pit of clay for to be made

     For such a guest is meet.

Ham. I think it be thine indeed, for thou liest in't.

Clown. You lie out on't, sir, and therefore 'tis not yours.

   For my part, I do not lie in't, yet it is mine.

Ham. Thou dost lie in't, to be in't and say it is thine. 'Tis for the dead, not for the quick; therefore thou liest.

Clown. 'Tis a quick lie, sir; 'twill away again from me to you.

Ham. What man dost thou dig it for?

Clown. For no man, sir.

Ham. What woman then?

Clown. For none neither.

Ham. Who is to be buried in't?

Clown. One that was a woman, sir; but, rest her soul, she's dead.

Ham. How absolute the knave is! We must speak by the card, or equivocation will undo us. By the Lord, Horatio, this three years I have taken note of it, the age is grown so picked that the too of the peasant comes so near the heel of the courtier he galls his kibe.- How long hast thou been a grave-maker?

Clown. Of all the days i' th' year, I came to't that day that our last king Hamlet overcame Fortinbras.

Ham. How long is that since?

Clown. Cannot you tell that? Every fool can tell that. It was the very day that young Hamlet was born- he that is mad, and sent into England.

Ham. Ay, marry, why was be sent into England?

Clown. Why, because 'a was mad. 'A shall recover his wits there; or, if 'a do not, 'tis no great matter there.

Ham. Why?

Clown. 'Twill not he seen in him there. There the men are as mad as he.

Ham. How came he mad?

Clown. Very strangely, they say.

Ham. How strangely?

Clown. Faith, e'en with losing his wits.

Ham. Upon what ground?

Clown. Why, here in Denmark. I have been sexton here, man and boy thirty years.

Ham. How long will a man lie i' th' earth ere he rot?

Clown. Faith, if 'a be not rotten before 'a die as we have many pocky corses now-a-days that will scarce hold the laying in,
I will last you some eight year or nine year. A tanner will last you nine year.

Ham. Why he more than another?

Clown. Why, sir, his hide is so tann'd with his trade that 'a will keep out water a great while; and your water is a sore decayer of your whoreson dead body. Here's a skull now. This skull hath lien you i' th' earth three-and-twenty years.

Ham. Whose was it?

Clown. A whoreson, mad fellow's it was. Whose do you think it was?

Ham. Nay, I know not.

Clown. A pestilence on him for a mad rogue! 'A pour'd a flagon of Rhenish on my head once. This same skull, sir, was Yorick's skull, the King's jester.

Ham. This?

Clown. E'en that.

Ham. Let me see. [Takes the skull.] Alas, poor Yorick! I knew him,

Horatio. A fellow of infinite jest, of most excellent fancy. He hath borne me on his back a thousand times. And now how abhorred in my imagination it is! My gorge rises at it. Here hung those lips that I have kiss'd I know not how oft. Where be your gibes now? your gambols? your songs? your flashes of merriment that were wont to set the table on a roar? Not one now, to mock your own grinning? Quite chap- fall'n? Now get you to my lady's chamber, and tell her, let her paint an inch thick, to this favour she must come. Make her laugh at that. Prithee, Horatio, tell me one thing.

Hor. What's that, my lord?

Ham. Dost thou think Alexander look'd o' this fashion i' th' earth?

Hor. E'en so.

Ham. And smelt so? Pah!

[Puts down the skull.]

Hor. E'en so, my lord.

Ham. To what base uses we may return, Horatio! Why may not imagination trace the noble dust of Alexander till he find it stopping a bunghole?

Hor. 'Twere to consider too curiously, to consider so.

Ham. No, faith, not a jot; but to follow him thither with modesty enough, and likelihood to lead it; as thus: Alexander died,

Alexander was buried, Alexander returneth into dust; the dust is earth; of earth we make loam; and why of that loam (whereto he was converted) might they not stop a beer barrel?

Imperious Caesar, dead and turn'd to clay,
Might stop a hole to keep the wind away.
O, that that earth which kept the world in awe
Should patch a wall t' expel the winter's flaw!

But soft! but soft! aside! Here comes the
King-

Enter [priests with] a coffin [in funeral
procession], King, Queen, Laertes, with Lords
attendant.]

The Queen, the courtiers. Who is this they
follow?
And with such maimed rites? This doth
betoken
The corse they follow did with desp'rate
hand
Fordo it own life. 'Twas of some estate.
Couch we awhile, and mark.

                              [Retires with Horatio.]

Laer. What ceremony else?
Ham. That is Laertes,
    A very noble youth. Mark.

Laer. What ceremony else?

Priest. Her obsequies have been as far enlarg'd

As we have warranty. Her death was doubtful;

And, but that great command o'ersways the order,

She should in ground unsanctified have lodg'd

Till the last trumpet. For charitable prayers,

Shards, flints, and pebbles should be thrown on her.

Yet here she is allow'd her virgin rites,

Her maiden strewments, and the bringing home

Of bell and burial.

Laer. Must there no more be done?

Priest. No more be done.

We should profane the service of the dead

To sing a requiem and such rest to her

As to peace-parted souls.

Laer. Lay her i' th' earth;

And from her fair and unpolluted flesh

May violets spring! I tell thee, churlish priest,

A minist'ring angel shall my sister be

When thou liest howling.

Ham. What, the fair Ophelia?

Queen. Sweets to the sweet! Farewell.

[Scatters flowers.]

I hop'd thou shouldst have been my Hamlet's wife;

I thought thy bride-bed to have deck'd, sweet maid,

And not have strew'd thy grave.

Laer. O, treble woe

Fall ten times treble on that cursed head

Whose wicked deed thy most ingenious sense

Depriv'd thee of! Hold off the earth awhile,

Till I have caught her once more in mine
arms.

Leaps in the grave.

Now pile your dust upon the quick and dead
Till of this flat a mountain you have made
T' o'ertop old Pelion or the skyish head
Of blue Olympus.

Ham. [comes forward] What is he whose grief
Bears such an emphasis? whose phrase of
sorrow
Conjures the wand'ring stars, and makes
them stand
Like wonder-wounded hearers? This is I,
Hamlet the Dane

.   *Leaps in after Laertes.*

Laer. The devil take thy soul!

[Grapples with him].

Ham. Thou pray'st not well.
I prithee take thy fingers from my throat;
For, though I am not splenitive and rash,

Yet have I in me something dangerous,

Which let thy wisdom fear. Hold off thy
hand!

King. Pluck them asunder.

Queen. Hamlet, Hamlet!

All. Gentlemen!

Hor. Good my lord, be quiet.

*[The Attendants part them, and they
come out of the grave.]*

Ham. Why, I will fight with him upon this
theme

Until my eyelids will no longer wag.

Queen. O my son, what theme?

Ham. I lov'd Ophelia. Forty thousand brothers

Could not (with all their quantity of love)

Make up my sum. What wilt thou do for her?

King. O, he is mad, Laertes.

Queen. For love of God, forbear him!

Ham. 'Swounds, show me what thou't do.

Woo't weep? woo't fight? woo't fast? woo't tear thyself?

Woo't drink up esill? eat a crocodile?

I'll do't. Dost thou come here to whine?

To outface me with leaping in her grave?

Be buried quick with her, and so will I.

And if thou prate of mountains, let them throw

Millions of acres on us, till our ground,

Singeing his pate against the burning zone,

Make Ossa like a wart! Nay, an thou'lt mouth,

I'll rant as well as thou.

Queen. This is mere madness;

And thus a while the fit will work on him.

Anon, as patient as the female dove

When that her golden couplets are disclos'd,

His silence will sit drooping.

Ham. Hear you, sir!

What is the reason that you use me thus?

I lov'd you ever. But it is no matter.

Let Hercules himself do what he may,

The cat will mew, and dog will have his day.
Exit.

King. I pray thee, good Horatio, wait upon
him.

Exit Horatio.

[To Laertes] Strengthen your patience in our
last night's
speech.

We'll put the matter to the present push.-

Good Gertrude, set some watch over your
son.-

This grave shall have a living monument.

An hour of quiet shortly shall we see;

Till then in patience our proceeding be.

Exeunt.

Scene II.

Elsinore. A hall in the Castle.

Enter Hamlet and Horatio.

  Ham. So much for this, sir; now shall you see
the other.
  You do remember all the circumstance?
  Hor. Remember it, my lord!
  Ham. Sir, in my heart there was a kind of
fighting
  That would not let me sleep. Methought I lay
  Worse than the mutinies in the bilboes.
Rashly-
  And prais'd be rashness for it; let us know,
  Our indiscretion sometime serves us well
  When our deep plots do pall; and that should
learn us
  There's a divinity that shapes our ends,

Rough-hew them how we will-

Hor. That is most certain.

Ham. Up from my cabin,

My sea-gown scarf'd about me, in the dark

Grop'd I to find out them; had my desire,

Finger'd their packet, and in fine withdrew

To mine own room again; making so bold

(My fears forgetting manners) to unseal

Their grand commission; where I found,
Horatio

(O royal knavery!), an exact command,

Larded with many several sorts of reasons,

Importing Denmark's health, and England's
too,

With, hoo! such bugs and goblins in my life-

That, on the supervise, no leisure bated,

No, not to stay the finding of the axe,

My head should be struck off.

Hor. Is't possible?

Ham. Here's the commission; read it at more leisure.

But wilt thou bear me how I did proceed?

Hor. I beseech you.

Ham. Being thus benetted round with villanies,

Or I could make a prologue to my brains,

They had begun the play. I sat me down;

Devis'd a new commission; wrote it fair.

I once did hold it, as our statists do,

A baseness to write fair, and labour'd much

How to forget that learning; but, sir, now

It did me yeoman's service. Wilt thou know

Th' effect of what I wrote?

Hor. Ay, good my lord.

Ham. An earnest conjuration from the King,

As England was his faithful tributary,

As love between them like the palm might flourish,

As peace should still her wheaten garland
wear

And stand a comma 'tween their amities,

And many such-like as's of great charge,

That, on the view and knowing of these
contents,

Without debatement further, more or less,

He should the bearers put to sudden death,

Not shriving time allow'd.

Hor. How was this seal'd?

Ham. Why, even in that was heaven ordinant.

I had my father's signet in my purse,

Which was the model of that Danish seal;

Folded the writ up in the form of th' other,

Subscrib'd it, gave't th' impression, plac'd it
safely,

The changeling never known. Now, the next
day

Was our sea-fight; and what to this was
sequent

Thou know'st already.

Hor. So Guildenstern and Rosencrantz go to't.

Ham. Why, man, they did make love to this
employment!

They are not near my conscience; their
defeat

Does by their own insinuation grow.

'Tis dangerous when the baser nature comes

Between the pass and fell incensed points

Of mighty opposites.

Hor. Why, what a king is this!

Ham. Does it not, thinks't thee, stand me now
upon-

He that hath kill'd my king, and whor'd my
mother;

Popp'd in between th' election and my
hopes;

Thrown out his angle for my proper life,

And with such coz'nage- is't not perfect
conscience

To quit him with this arm? And is't not to be damn'd

To let this canker of our nature come

In further evil?

Hor. It must be shortly known to him from England

What is the issue of the business there.

Ham. It will be short; the interim is mine,

And a man's life is no more than to say 'one.'

But I am very sorry, good Horatio,

That to Laertes I forgot myself,

For by the image of my cause I see

The portraiture of his. I'll court his favours.

But sure the bravery of his grief did put me

Into a tow'ring passion.

Hor. Peace! Who comes here?

Enter young Osric, a courtier.

Osr. Your lordship is right welcome back to Denmark.

Ham. I humbly thank you, sir. [Aside to Horatio] Dost know this waterfly?

Hor. [aside to Hamlet] No, my good lord.

Ham. [aside to Horatio] Thy state is the more gracious; for 'tis a vice to know him. He hath much land, and fertile. Let a beast be lord of beasts, and his crib shall stand at the king's mess. Tis a chough; but, as I say, spacious in the possession of dirt.

Osr. Sweet lord, if your lordship were at leisure, I should impart

a thing to you from his Majesty.

Ham. I will receive it, sir, with all diligence of spirit. Put your bonnet to his right use. 'Tis for the head.

Osr. I thank your lordship, it is very hot.

Ham. No, believe me, 'tis very cold; the wind is northerly.

Osr. It is indifferent cold, my lord, indeed.

Ham. But yet methinks it is very sultry and hot for my complexion.

Osr. Exceedingly, my lord; it is very sultry, as 'twere- I cannot tell how. But, my lord, his Majesty bade me signify to you that he has laid a great wager on your head. Sir, this is the matter-

Ham. I beseech you remember.

[Hamlet moves him to put on his hat.]

Osr. Nay, good my lord; for mine ease, in good faith. Sir, here is newly come to court Laertes; believe me, an absolute gentleman, full of most excellent differences, of very soft society and great showing. Indeed, to speak feelingly of him, he is the card or calendar of gentry; for you shall find in him the continent of what part a gentleman would see.

Ham. Sir, his definement suffers no perdition in you; though, I know, to divide him inventorially would dozy th' arithmetic of memory, and yet but yaw neither in respect of his quick sail.

But, in the verity of extolment, I take him to be a soul of great article, and his infusion of such dearth and rareness as, to make true diction of him, his semblable is his mirror, and who else would trace him, his umbrage, nothing more.

Osr. Your lordship speaks most infallibly of him.

Ham. The concernancy, sir? Why do we wrap the gentleman in our more rawer breath?

Osr. Sir?

Hor [aside to Hamlet] Is't not possible to understand in another tongue? You will do't, sir, really.

Ham. What imports the nomination of this gentleman?

Osr. Of Laertes?

Hor. [aside] His purse is empty already. All's golden words are spent.

Ham. Of him, sir.

Osr. I know you are not ignorant-

Ham. I would you did, sir; yet, in faith, if you did, it would not much approve me. Well, sir?

Osr. You are not ignorant of what excellence Laertes is-

Ham. I dare not confess that, lest I should compare with him in excellence; but to know a man well were to know himself.

Osr. I mean, sir, for his weapon; but in the imputation laid on him

by them, in his meed he's unfellowed.

Ham. What's his weapon?

Osr. Rapier and dagger.

Ham. That's two of his weapons- but well.

Osr. The King, sir, hath wager'd with him six Barbary horses; against the which he has impon'd, as I take it, six French rapiers and poniards, with their assigns, as girdle, hangers, and so. Three of the carriages, in faith, are very dear to fancy, very responsive to the hilts, most delicate carriages, and of very liberal conceit.

Ham. What call you the carriages?

Hor. [aside to Hamlet] I knew you must be edified by the margent ere you had done.

Osr. The carriages, sir, are the hangers.

Ham. The phrase would be more germane to the matter if we could carry cannon by our sides. I would it might be hangers till then.

But on! Six Barbary horses against six French swords, their assigns, and three liberal-conceited carriages: that's the French bet against the Danish. Why is this all impon'd, as you call it?

Osr. The King, sir, hath laid that, in a dozen passes between yourself and him, he shall not exceed you three hits; he hath laid on twelve for nine, and it would come to immediate trial if your lordship would vouchsafe the answer.

Ham. How if I answer no?

Osr. I mean, my lord, the opposition of your person in trial.

Ham. Sir, I will walk here in the hall. If it please his Majesty, it is the breathing time of day with me. Let the foils be brought, the gentleman willing, and the King hold his purpose, I will win for him if I can; if not, I will gain nothing but my shame and the odd hits.

Osr. Shall I redeliver you e'en so?

Ham. To this effect, sir, after what flourish your nature will.

Osr. I commend my duty to your lordship.

Ham. Yours, yours.

[Exit Osric.]

He does well to commend it himself; there are no tongues else for's turn.

Hor. This lapwing runs away with the shell on his head.

Ham. He did comply with his dug before he suck'd it. Thus has he, and many more of the same bevy that I know the drossy age dotes on, only got the tune of the time and outward habit of encounter- a kind of yesty collection, which carries them through and through the most fann'd and winnowed opinions; and do but blow them to their trial-the bubbles are out,

Enter a Lord.

Lord. My lord, his Majesty commended him to you by young Osric, who brings back to him, that you attend him in the hall. He sends to know if your pleasure hold to play with

Laertes, or that you will take longer time.

Ham. I am constant to my purposes; they

follow the King's pleasure.

If his fitness speaks, mine is ready; now or

whensoever, provided

I be so able as now.

Lord. The King and Queen and all are coming

down.

Ham. In happy time.

Lord. The Queen desires you to use some

gentle entertainment to

Laertes before you fall to play.

Ham. She well instructs me.

[Exit Lord.]

Hor. You will lose this wager, my lord.

Ham. I do not think so. Since he went into

France I have been in continual practice. I shall

win at the odds. But thou wouldst not think

how ill all's here about my heart. But it is no matter.

Hor. Nay, good my lord -

Ham. It is but foolery; but it is such a kind of gaingiving as would perhaps trouble a woman.

Hor. If your mind dislike anything, obey it. I will forestall their repair hither and say you are not fit.

Ham. Not a whit, we defy augury; there's a special providence in the fall of a sparrow. If it be now, 'tis not to come; if it be not to come, it will be now; if it be not now, yet it will come: the readiness is all. Since no man knows aught of what he leaves, what is't to leave betimes? Let be.

Enter King, Queen, Laertes, Osric, and Lords, with other Attendants with foils and gauntlets. A table and flagons of wine on it.

King. Come, Hamlet, come, and take this hand from me.

The King puts Laertes' hand into Hamlet's.]

Ham. Give me your pardon, sir. I have done you wrong;

But pardon't, as you are a gentleman.

This presence knows,

And you must needs have heard, how I am punish'd

With sore distraction. What I have done

That might your nature, honour, and exception

Roughly awake, I here proclaim was madness.

Was't Hamlet wrong'd Laertes? Never Hamlet.

If Hamlet from himself be taken away,

And when he's not himself does wrong Laertes,

Then Hamlet does it not, Hamlet denies it.

Who does it, then? His madness. If't be so,

Hamlet is of the faction that is wrong'd;

His madness is poor Hamlet's enemy.

Sir, in this audience,

Let my disclaiming from a purpos'd evil

Free me so far in your most generous

thoughts

That I have shot my arrow o'er the house

And hurt my brother.

Laer. I am satisfied in nature,

Whose motive in this case should stir me

most

To my revenge. But in my terms of honour

I stand aloof, and will no reconcilement

Till by some elder masters of known honour

I have a voice and precedent of peace

To keep my name ungor'd. But till that time

I do receive your offer'd love like love,

And will not wrong it.

Ham. I embrace it freely,

And will this brother's wager frankly play.

Give us the foils. Come on.

Laer. Come, one for me.

Ham. I'll be your foil, Laertes. In mine ignorance

Your skill shall, like a star i' th' darkest night,

Stick fiery off indeed.

Laer. You mock me, sir.

Ham. No, by this hand.

King. Give them the foils, young Osric. Cousin Hamlet,

You know the wager?

Ham. Very well, my lord.

Your Grace has laid the odds o' th' weaker side.

King. I do not fear it, I have seen you both;

But since he is better'd, we have therefore odds.

Laer. This is too heavy; let me see another.

Ham. This likes me well. These foils have all a length?

Prepare to play.

Osr. Ay, my good lord.

King. Set me the stoups of wine upon that table.

If Hamlet give the first or second hit,

Or quit in answer of the third exchange,

Let all the battlements their ordnance fire;

The King shall drink to Hamlet's better breath,

And in the cup an union shall he throw

Richer than that which four successive kings

In Denmark's crown have worn. Give me the cups;

And let the kettle to the trumpet speak,

The trumpet to the cannoneer without,

The cannons to the heavens, the heaven to earth,

'Now the King drinks to Hamlet.' Come, begin.

And you the judges, bear a wary eye.

Ham. Come on, sir.

Laer. Come, my lord

.   *They play.*

Ham. One.

Laer. No.

Ham. Judgment!

Osr. A hit, a very palpable hit.

Laer. Well, again!

King. Stay, give me drink. Hamlet, this pearl is thine;

Here's to thy health.

          [Drum; trumpets sound; a piece goes off [within].

Give him the cup.

Ham. I'll play this bout first; set it by awhile.

Come. (They play.) Another hit. What say you?

Laer. A touch, a touch; I do confess't.

King. Our son shall win.

Queen. He's fat, and scant of breath.

Here, Hamlet, take my napkin, rub thy brows.

The Queen carouses to thy fortune, Hamlet.

Ham. Good madam!

King. Gertrude, do not drink.

Queen. I will, my lord; I pray you pardon me.

Drinks.

King. [aside] It is the poison'd cup; it is too late.

Ham. I dare not drink yet, madam; by-and-by.

Queen. Come, let me wipe thy face.

Laer. My lord, I'll hit him now.

King. I do not think't.

Laer. [aside] And yet it is almost against my conscience.

Ham. Come for the third, Laertes! You but dally.

Pray you pass with your best violence;

I am afeard you make a wanton of me.

Laer. Say you so? Come on.

Play.

Osr. Nothing neither way.

Laer. Have at you now!

[Laertes wounds Hamlet; then] in scuffling, they change rapiers, [and Hamlet wounds Laertes].

King. Part them! They are incens'd.

Ham. Nay come! again!

The Queen falls.

Osr. Look to the Queen there, ho!

Hor. They bleed on both sides. How is it, my lord?

Osr. How is't, Laertes?

Laer. Why, as a woodcock to mine own springe, Osric.

I am justly kill'd with mine own treachery.

Ham. How does the Queen?

King. She sounds to see them bleed.

Queen. No, no! the drink, the drink! O my dear Hamlet!

The drink, the drink! I am poison'd.

[Dies.]

Ham. O villany! Ho! let the door be lock'd.

Treachery! Seek it out.

[Laertes falls.]

Laer. It is here, Hamlet. Hamlet, thou art slain;

No medicine in the world can do thee good.

In thee there is not half an hour of life.

The treacherous instrument is in thy hand,

Unbated and envenom'd. The foul practice

Hath turn'd itself on me. Lo, here I lie,

Never to rise again. Thy mother's poison'd.

I can no more. The King, the King's to blame.

Ham. The point envenom'd too?

Then, venom, to thy work.

Hurts the King.

All. Treason! treason!

King. O, yet defend me, friends! I am but hurt.

Ham. Here, thou incestuous, murd'rous,
damned Dane,

Drink off this potion! Is thy union here?

Follow my mother.

King dies.

Laer. He is justly serv'd.

It is a poison temper'd by himself.

Exchange forgiveness with me, noble
Hamlet.

Mine and my father's death come not upon
thee,

Nor thine on me!

Dies.

Ham. Heaven make thee free of it! I follow
thee.

I am dead, Horatio. Wretched queen, adieu!

You that look pale and tremble at this
chance,

That are but mutes or audience to this act,

Had I but time (as this fell sergeant, Death,

Is strict in his arrest) O, I could tell you-

But let it be. Horatio, I am dead;

Thou liv'st; report me and my cause aright

To the unsatisfied.

Hor. Never believe it.

I am more an antique Roman than a Dane.

Here's yet some liquor left.

Ham. As th'art a man,

Give me the cup. Let go! By heaven, I'll ha't.

O good Horatio, what a wounded name

(Things standing thus unknown) shall live

behind me!

If thou didst ever hold me in thy heart,

Absent thee from felicity awhile,

And in this harsh world draw thy breath in

pain,

To tell my story.

[March afar off, and shot within.]

What warlike noise is this?

Osr. Young Fortinbras, with conquest come from Poland,

To the ambassadors of England gives

This warlike volley.

Ham. O, I die, Horatio!

The potent poison quite o'ercrows my spirit.

I cannot live to hear the news from England,

But I do prophesy th' election lights

On Fortinbras. He has my dying voice.

So tell him, with th' occurrents, more and less,

Which have solicited- the rest is silence.

Dies.

Hor. Now cracks a noble heart. Good night, sweet prince,

And flights of angels sing thee to thy rest!

[March within.]

Why does the drum come hither?

Enter Fortinbras and English Ambassadors,
with Drum, Colours, and Attendants.

Fort. Where is this sight?

Hor. What is it you will see?

If aught of woe or wonder, cease your
search.

Fort. This quarry cries on havoc. O proud
Death,

What feast is toward in thine eternal cell

That thou so many princes at a shot

So bloodily hast struck.

Ambassador. The sight is dismal;

And our affairs from England come too late.

The ears are senseless that should give us
hearing

To tell him his commandment is fulfill'd

That Rosencrantz and Guildenstern are
dead.

Where should we have our thanks?

Hor. Not from his mouth,

    Had it th' ability of life to thank you.

    He never gave commandment for their
death.

    But since, so jump upon this bloody
question,

    You from the Polack wars, and you from
England,

    Are here arriv'd, give order that these bodies

    High on a stage be placed to the view;

    And let me speak to the yet unknowing
world

    How these things came about. So shall you
hear

    Of carnal, bloody and unnatural acts;

    Of accidental judgments, casual slaughters;

    Of deaths put on by cunning and forc'd
cause;

    And, in this upshot, purposes mistook

    Fall'n on th' inventors' heads. All this can I

Truly deliver.

Fort. Let us haste to hear it,

And call the noblest to the audience.

For me, with sorrow I embrace my fortune.

I have some rights of memory in this kingdom

Which now, to claim my vantage doth invite me.

Hor. Of that I shall have also cause to speak,

And from his mouth whose voice will draw on more.

But let this same be presently perform'd,

Even while men's minds are wild, lest more mischance

On plots and errors happen.

Fort. Let four captains

Bear Hamlet like a soldier to the stage;

For he was likely, had he been put on,

To have prov'd most royally; and for his passage

The soldiers' music and the rites of war

Speak loudly for him.

Take up the bodies. Such a sight as this

Becomes the field but here shows much
amiss.

Go, bid the soldiers shoot.

*Exeunt marching; after the which a peal
of ordnance are shot off.*

THE END.

Made in the USA
Coppell, TX
05 September 2021